99 DOMES

IBRAHIM MOHAMED JAIDAH

99 DOMES

MASJID OF IMAM MUHAMMAD IBN ABDUL WAHHAB

SKIRA

Author & Masjid's Lead Designer
Ibrahim Mohamed Jaidah
Group CEO and Chief Architect
Arab Engineering Bureau

Peer review and Validation
Dr. Ali A. Alraouf
Professor of Architecture
& Urbanism
Head of Development, Research
and Capacity Building

Content Management and Project
Coordination
Lejla Nikšić

Research and Architectural Drawings
Fatma Abdullah Khalfani

Sketches
Fatma Abdullah Khalfani
Wesam Roshdy Gad

Interior Design
Wesam Roshdy Gad

Photographers
Abdullah Hamdan Al-Mannai
Yousef Mubarak Al-Dossari
Fernando R. Doria
Oliver A. Sumampong
Ruel C. Fulache
Zandro E. Sardinia

Project Sponsored by
Qatar Museums (QM)

Coordination and Project Initiative
Noof Ibrahim Hassan Al-Abdulla
Director of Publications Department
Qatar Museums (QM)

Cover
View from the southern outdoor corridor
(*riwaq*) toward the
north-eastern side of the courtyard
where the minaret is placed

Back Cover
The shadow of patterned brass
metallic screen ornates the flooring
of the inner space of the *riwaq*
and hallways

Design
Marcello Francone

Editorial Coordination
Emma Cavazzini

Editing
Ondina Granato

Layout
Antonio Carminati

First published in Italy in 2015 by
Skira editore S.p.A.
Palazzo Casati Stampa
via Torino 61
20123 Milano
Italy
www.skira.net

Printed and bound in Italy. First edition

ISBN: 978-88-572-2278-3

Distributed in USA, Canada,
Central & South America by Rizzoli
International Publications, Inc.,
300 Park Avenue South, New York,
NY 10010, USA.
Distributed elsewhere in the world
by Thames and Hudson Ltd.,
181A High Holborn, London WC1V 7QX,
United Kingdom.

Design

Main Building Architect
Mimar consult

Main Consultant
AEB

Architectural Design Development
AEB

Covered Car Park and Podium Design
AEB

MEP Consultant
Shaker Consultancy Group

Lighting Design
Shld Architectural Lighting Designs

Interior Design
AEB

Landscape Design
AEB

Traffic
Trafictich

Construction

Project Management and Construction Supervision
AEB

Main Contractor
Contraco

Joinery Work
El-Misned

Brass Work
CREART (Creative Art Group)

بسم الله الرحمن الرحيم

In the Name of Allah, the Most Gracious, the Most Merciful

Acknowledgement and Dedication

It is not only a great honor to be commissioned to do a landmark, but it is an important responsibility especially as that landmark will become a reference for generations to come. Therefore I would like to thank the government of State of Qatar and Private Engineering Office for giving me this opportunity in playing a major role in design of this and other major landmarks that reflect the true identity of a modern Qatar.

I would also like to thank a distinguished group of individuals who aided me as an author in publishing of this book.

Special thanks go to Qatar Museums (QM) and Noof Ibrahim Hassan Al-Abdulla, Director of Publications Department, for their initiative and gracious support in the development of this publication. I am particularly grateful for the assistance of my team from AEB – Lejla Nikšić, Fatma Abdullah Khalfani, and Wesam Roshdy Gad – for their efforts and contributions in bringing together this book.

To the great architect AlHumaili who created a masterpiece of the original AlQubeib mosque.
And to old masons who aided AlHumaili in building the original mosque.

To my mentor, my dear mother.

Ibrahim Jaidah

The Leader's Vision

We live in a fast changing world where unfortunately – due to the globalization – cultures, traditions, customs, and even languages of many places and nations are vanishing.

Under the rule of HH The Father Emir Sheikh Hamad bin Khalifa Al Thani, Qatar considerably reflected on its heritage and identity. The survival of the local identity became of paramount importance in the State that was developing at such fast rate. HH Sheikh Hamad bin Khalifa Al Thani encouraged us all to reflect on our past and go back to our roots. This marked a comeback of traditional arts and architecture, a new renaissance in the approach to modernism with a strong base in the culture.

Being open minded towards the future of his State and his people, HH Sheikh Hamad bin Khalifa Al Thani encouraged the building of the State's mosque that will stand as a landmark in the modern State of Qatar and at the same time will exist in the context of local culture and tradition.

If a picture could say 1000 words,
the one on the left truly reflects
a vision of a leader where with
presence of strong identity,
we venture into the future

Contents

14 **Introduction**

16 Book Vision and Structure
17 History and Architecture of Mosques in Qatar
17 *Traditional Qatari Architecture*
18 *Mosques in Qatar*

Chapter I
26 **Evolution of Multi-domed Mosques**

27 Chronological Phases of Multi-domed Mosques in Qatar
29 *End of the 18th Century*
29 *End of the 19th Century*
29 *Mid-End of the 20th Century*
31 The New State Mosque
34 Naming of the Mosque
34 *The* masjid *of Imam Muhammad ibn Abdul Wahhab*
34 Short Biography of Imam Muhammad ibn Abdul Wahhab

Chapter II
38 **The Language of Architecture**

39 Urban Geography: Site and Context
40 Design Concept and Building Form
40 The Language of Architecture
44 *Aesthetic Values and Principles*
44 *Style and Form*
64 *Lighting*
87 *Materials*
95 *Statistics and Technical Aspects of the Mosque*

Chapter III
96 **Poetics of Architecture: Elements of the Masjid**

106 *Musalla*
106 *Sahn*
106 *Riwaq*
118 *Mihrab*
118 *Minbar*
122 Minaret
122 Library and Reading Area
135 *Mutawada'a*
135 *Sabeel*
139 *Masjid*'s Building Structure
139 *Arcades (Columns and Arches)*
139 *The Significance of 99 Domes*

Chapter IV
148 **Artistic and Aesthetic Values of the Masjid**

149 The Link between Art and Architecture in Islam
155 Openings: Doors, Windows and Screens
155 Geometrical Patterns and Calligraphy

Conclusion
184 **Epilogue**

185 The Significance of Imam Muhammad ibn Abdul Wahhab Masjid
191 The *Masjid*'s Contribution to Qatari Architecture and Local Identity

Appendix
192 Glossary
196 Bibliography and Selected References

Introduction

In a world where the magnificence of Islam and all its physical and nonphysical manifestations are shadowed by fear, creativity should speak to the truth of this religion. Almost all researchers and scholars on the topic of Islamic art and architecture agreed upon the fact that the mosque is the most influential component in the fabric of any Islamic city (Serageldin, 1996; Frishman, 1994). Throughout the different eras of Islamic history, the mosque was – and remains – a convergence center and meeting point for not only worshipers but the whole wider community. The mosque has continuously played a vital role in the guidance of the Muslim community, being used as *quranic madrasa* and center for Islamic education, teaching both the young and older generations as well as becoming a place for Muslims to meet on religious occasions. The mosque has acted as a social, cultural, and even political center. Architecture and urbanism, as numerous researchers have suggested, used to be the physical representation of Muslim communities' abilities, creativity, and positive contributions in mankind development (AlHahtlul, 1981; Hakim, 1986; Mortada, 2003). The example of the mosque is rather important since it is not only an Islamic building but a physical representation of ideology (Alraouf, 2011). It is the place where the main pillar of Islam religion, Prayer, is performed five times a day.

> "Traditional Islamic civilization is marked by its emphasize upon beauty being wedded to every aspect of human life, from the chanting of the *Qur'an* to the making of pots and pans. The traditional Islamic ambience, both the plastic and the sonoral, have always been beautiful, for traditional Islam sees beauty as a complement of the Truth."
> Nasr (1990) p. 20

The history and development of the mosque since the time of the Prophet Muhammad explain its traditional religious and teaching role in Muslim society as well as its architectural and decorative features. He argued that the mosque had become the physical expression of belief in Allah and a signal of submission to Allah's will. The physical form of the mosque when analyzed would reveal that main elements were repeatedly used in its design due to their symbolic importance. Elements like domes, vaults, arches, arcades, traditional ornamentation, and pure forms in addition to minarets were becoming essential in most of mosques design (Alraouf, 2011; 2014).

On a city planning level, traditional Islamic cities organically grew around the mosque. It was simply the genesis of the city, physically and symbolically. On an architectural level, the mosque was and still is a manifestation of the Islamic creativity in art, calligraphy, geometry and all other forms of art and architecture. The mosques were the most important architectural structures in the Islamic civilization, inspiring all the further Islamic architectural style through distinctive spatial qualities and experiences. As a building type, the mosque introduced unique architectural elements such as domes, vaults, courtyards, gates, corridors, arches, columns, and pillars. The architecture of the mosques balances poetically between the magnificence of the monumental design and the deliberate respect of human scale spaces. Without any doubt, the mosques are the types of buildings in Islamic world where the connection between the concepts of form and content is most evident.

Book Vision and Structure

The main concept of the book emerged from a compiling desire to share a long creative journey to design and build one of the most visible and valuable additions to the contemporary urbanity of Qatar, the mosque of Imam Muhammad ibn Abdul Wahhab. Hence, the book presents, in an illustrative form, both artistic and architectural details of the Qatar state's grand mosque. It narrates the special experience of creating the biggest mosque in the State of Qatar, named after the Imam Muhammad ibn Abdul Wahhab and adorned by astonishing 99 domes. The book takes the reader on a rich visual and spatial journey within and around the *masjid*, highlighting its design intricacies which merge magnificence and simplicity in an unique harmony. The philosophy of the book is to rest fundamentally on visual materials and make the text as a secondary yet explanatory component of the structure of the book.

The book is divided into introduction, four chapters, conclusion and an appendix with a glossary and a selected bibliography. The first section is an introduction to the evolution of mosques architecture in Qatar, explaining chronologically the changes that occurred to the construction and layout planning of the mosques. Following chapters describe in details different aspects of the mosque design including its main features, the 99 domes. The first chapter briefly outlines the historical evolution of multi-domed mosques in Qatar reaching to the present time and more specifically explains the history behind the construction of the state mosque and the reasoning for naming it after the Imam. Chapter two literally describes the location, geography and urban situation of the mosque. It also describes the anatomy of architecture, the conceptual development of the building form, and the technical aspects of the mosque. Conversely, the third chapter focuses on the elements and components of the mosque by describing the building structure. The fourth chapter focuses on the details and exceptional art features of the mosque, decoding more precisely the interior particulars of the mosque, concentrating on the patterns, ornaments, calligraphy, and specific details of the wooden and iron doors and screens. The final section of this book, the conclusion, explains the mosque's importance as an outstanding landmark and the value it adds to the city's identity and local architecture. At the end of the book, a glossary of traditional and mosque architecture is provided. A list of references and a selected bibliography are also included for readers who are interested to gain more knowledge about such unique buildings in Islamic architecture.

History and Architecture of Mosques in Qatar

Traditional Qatari Architecture

Muslim communities are continually balancing the essence of their faith with the diversity of geography, politics, cultures, and economies (AlHathul, 2004). Traditional architecture in the Gulf and precisely in Qatar was a brilliant response to the different contextual challenges. The traditional Qatari architecture evolved not only as an adaptation to socio-cultural shifts but also as a response to the harsh environment: drifting sands, sparse dry hills, scant rain and hot desert winds. Traditionally, social and cultural factors were so dominating in shaping the forms of cities and buildings alike around the Gulf cities and settlements. Crucial principles emerged from the social and cultural context and substantially affected the built environment. In the book *The History of Qatari Architecture 1800-1950*, Qatari architecture is described as a society-based architecture that primarily satisfies the social, cultural and spiritual needs of the community such as family growth, privacy, and religion. Additionally, the local climate and weather patterns of the region are considered to have the most predominant influence on the design upon which the urban fabric and buildings have been shaped (Jaidah and Bourennane, 2009). Traditionally the domestic houses were introverted, with rough, thick exterior walls that preserved privacy and protected against sand storms. The inside featured formal geometric patterns with a central courtyard and serene gardens that were laid out to maximize shade, helping maintain a temperate interior and achieve the needed family privacy. The traditional Qatari architecture is known for its simplicity in both form and ornamentation, particularly if compared with the rest of the Arabian Gulf architecture. This is predominantly true in the case of the mosques, as they had been humbly created through the simplicity of design.

Mosques in Qatar

As mosques are a manifestation of the Islamic ideology, it is essential to hint to how Islam became the main religion in the Gulf context. Islam spread across the entire Arabian region in the 7th century AD in a string of widespread conflicts resulting in the native Arabian pagans converting to Islam. With the spread of Islam in Qatar, Prophet Muhammad (peace be upon him) sent his first military envoy, led by Al Ala AlHadrami, to AlMunzir ibn Sawi AlTamimi, the ruler of Bahrain, which extended from the coast of Kuwait to the south of Qatar, including AlHasa and Bahrain. Precisely, in the year 628 AD, Prophet Muhammad (peace be upon him) invited AlMunzir to convert to Islam, just as he had invited other kingdoms and empires of his time including Byzantium and Persia. AlMunzir responded positively to Prophet Muhammad (peace be upon him) by declaring his acceptance of Islam, and all the inhabitants of the area under his rule became Muslim, heralding the beginning of the Islamic era in Qatar.

With the spread of Islam as a religion in the region, the extensive construction of mosques started following the model of the very first mosque, which was the courtyard of Prophet Muhammad's (peace be upon him) house in Medina, constructed in 622 AD. The Prophet's (peace be upon him) house in Medina, in modern-day Saudi Arabia, was a typical 7th century Arabian style house with a courtyard surrounded by long rooms supported by columns. This is where the hypostyle – meaning many columns – mosque style evolved from. Most mosques built in the region utilized this style for centuries. The Prophet's (peace be upon him) house was organized with a *qibla*, initially facing in the direction of Jerusalem. There were three entrances to the courtyard. An area of the courtyard was roofed, and in here the prayer was performed. Later, the *qibla* was changed, facing Mecca.

1.
Remains of the very first mosque in Qatar located in Murwab archaeological site. Qatar Museums, 2015

2.
The reconstruction layout of the Prophet's House, Medina, Saudi Arabia

4.
Layout of AlQubeib (Sheikh Jassim bin Muhammed) Mosque in Doha, an example of the second type of layout of the early mosques of Qatar.
Khadrawi, 2009

3.
Layout of Ein Sinan Mosque in the northern side of Qatar, 1 940, an example of the first type of layout of the early mosques of Qatar.
Khadrawi, 2009

5.
Layout of AlKhuweir Mosque, an example of the third type of layout of the early mosques of Qatar.
Khadrawi, 2009

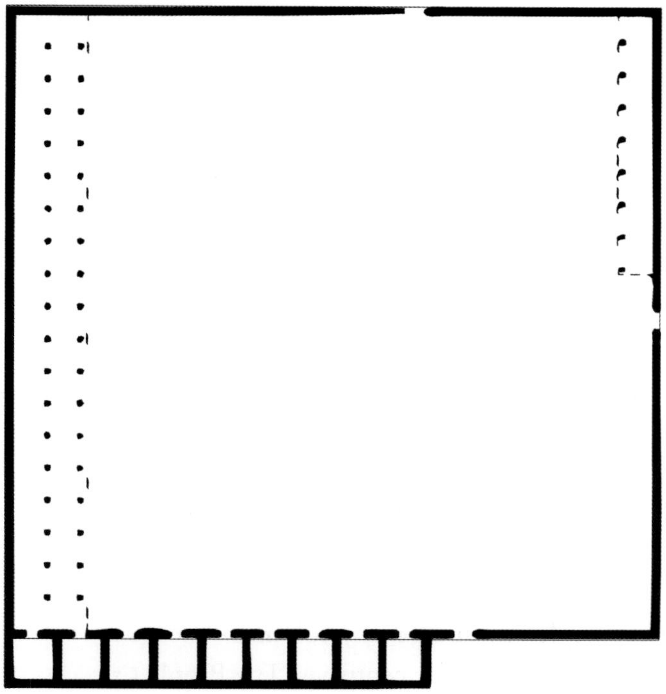

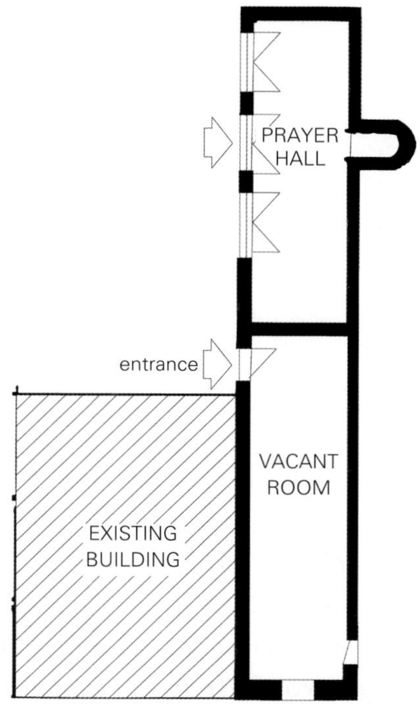

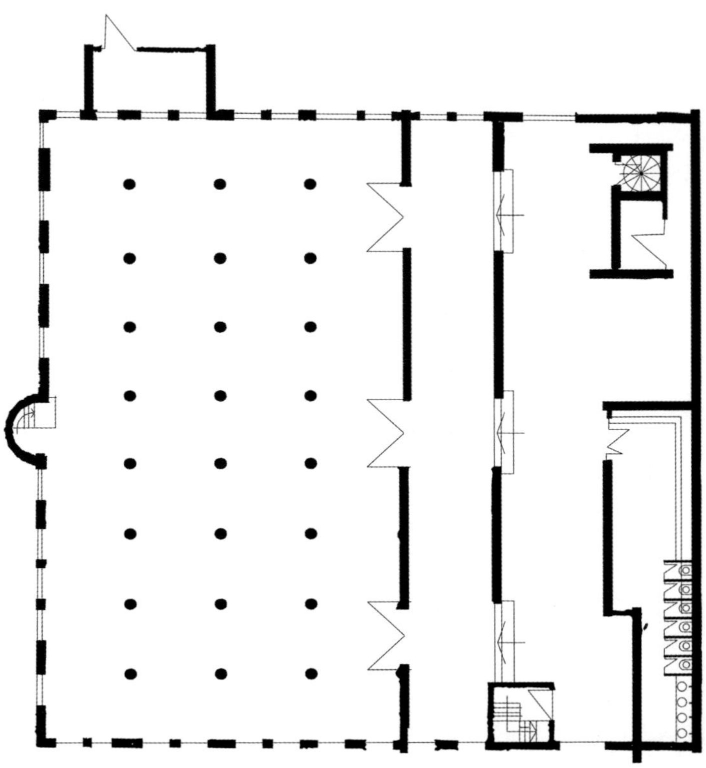

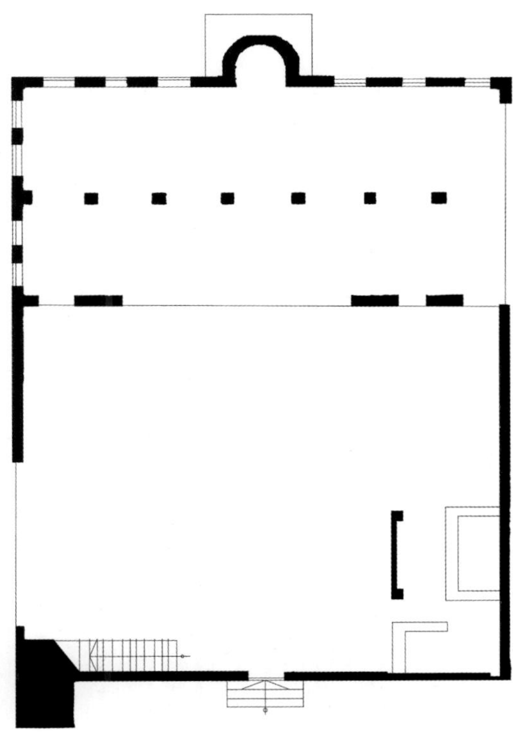

6.
AlYousef Mosque built in 1940 following the third type of layout of the early mosques of Qatar.
Jaidah & Bourennane, 2009

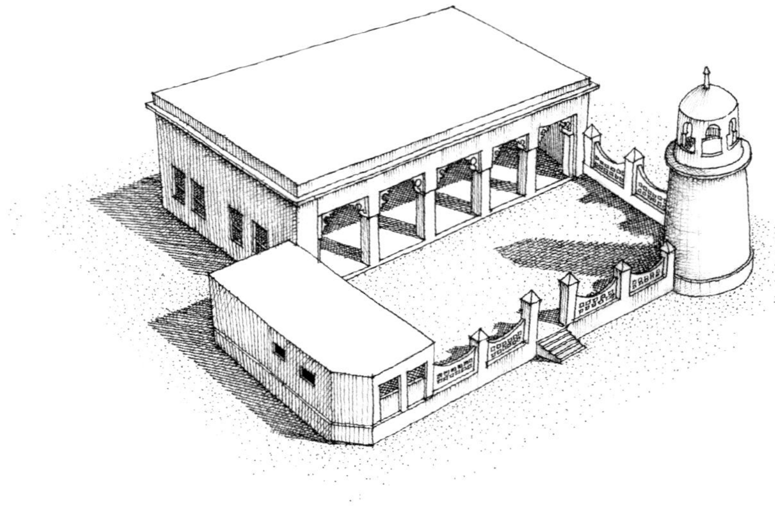

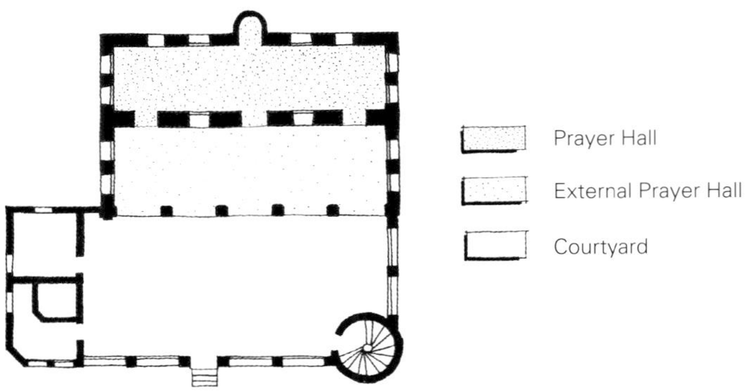

Plan

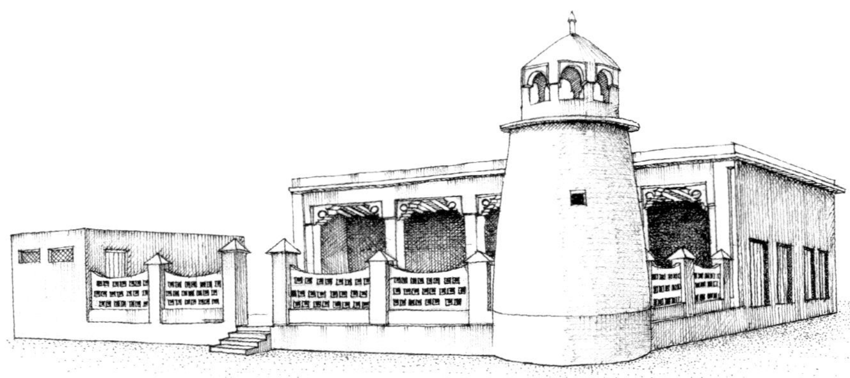

7.
Zekreet Mosque built in 1940 following the third type of layout of the early mosques of Qatar.
Jaidah & Bourennane, 2009

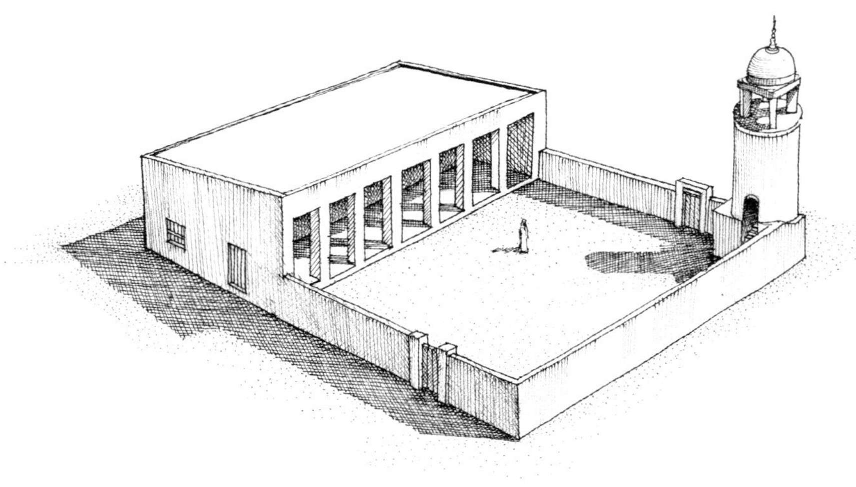

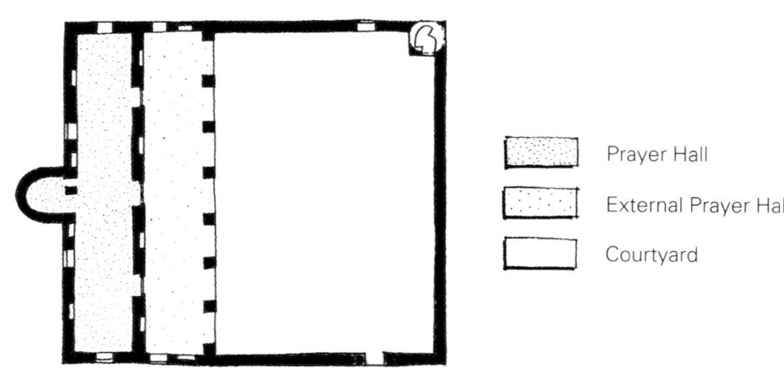

Floor Plan

8.
AlKhotba Mosque at AlDukhan built in 1943 following the third type of layout of the early mosques of Qatar. Jaidah & Bourennane, 2009

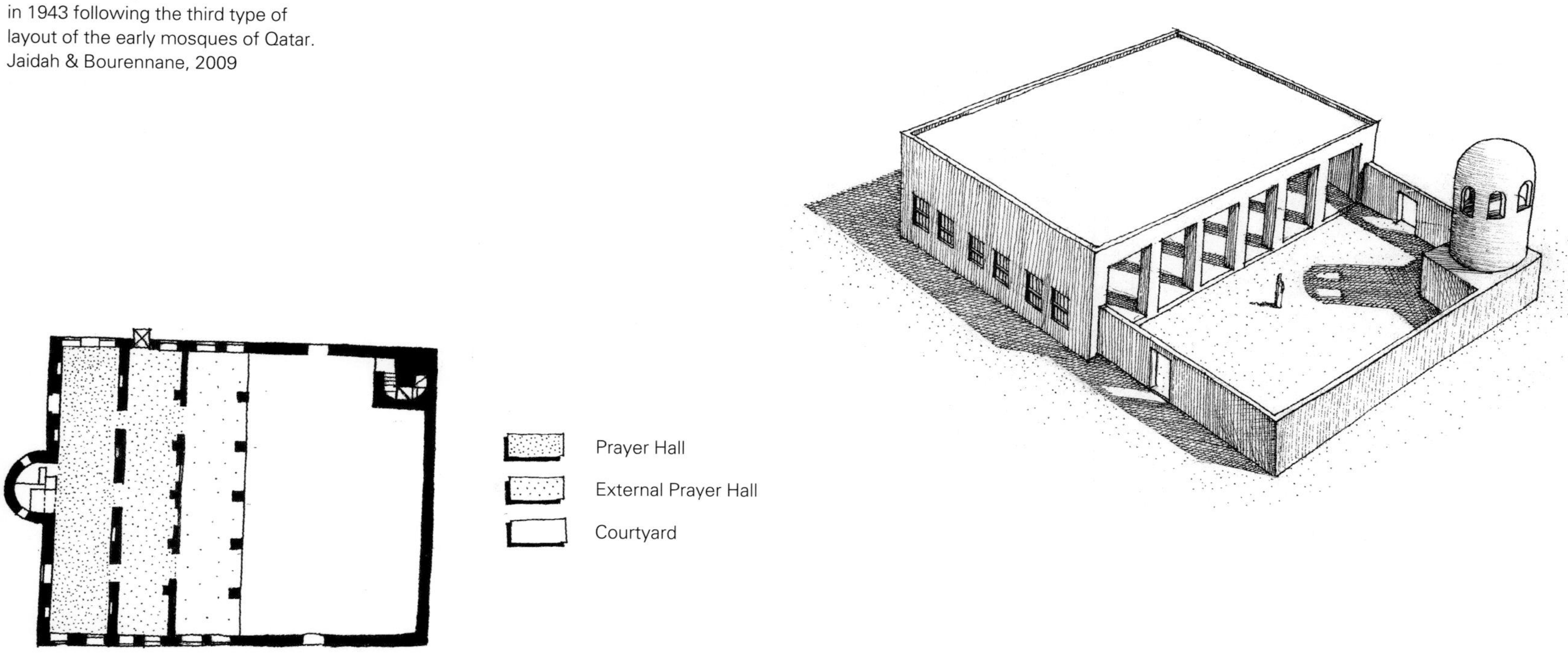

9.
Old Mosque at Rawdat Rashid built in 1948 following the third type of layout of the early mosques of Qatar. Jaidah & Bourennane, 2009

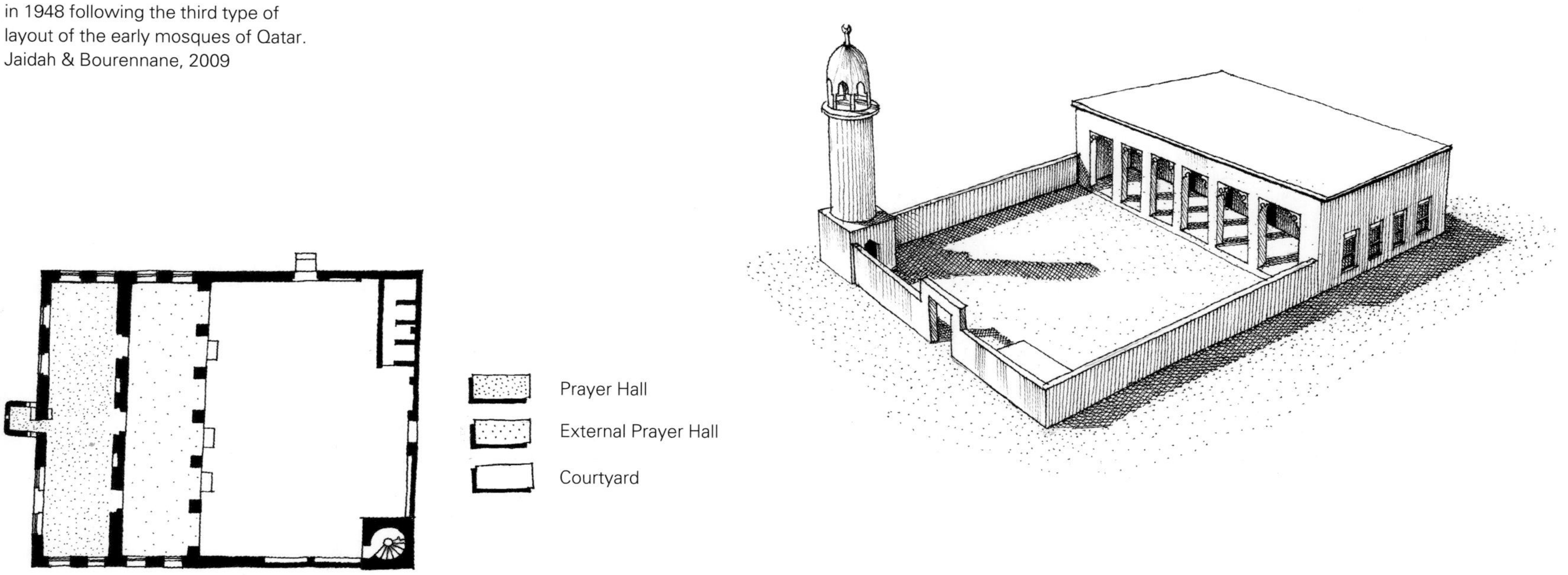

Within few years after the death of Prophet Muhammad (peace be upon him), mosques became such important symbols, that when Muslim conquerors attained new territories, a mosque was put up first, and then the military camp was built around it. This was inspired by the Medina example, but in some principal cities, Muslims constructed their mosque in the place of worship for other religions.

The early mosques were traditionally uncomplicated, simple in their design. However, mosques soon grew into more complex structures. The architecture of mosques was most strongly influenced by the traditions of the time and by the place where they were built. As a result, style, layout, and decoration of historic mosques vary greatly. Nevertheless, because of the common function of the mosque as a place of congregational prayer, certain architectural features and elements such as *mihrab*, *minbar*, *riwaq* and the minaret appear in mosques all over the world.

With the spread of Islam, unique styles have inevitably evolved and the construction of the mosques and other sacred buildings showed that the Islamic architecture has been transported, transformed and influenced by variety of architectural styles from around the world. Islamic architecture first emerged as a distinct style with the reconstruction of the holy sanctuary of Ka'ba in the city of Mecca that was rebuilt in Abbasid style, familiar to the builder who undertook the work. Hence, the architecture of the mosques merged a range of artistic styles of the concurred regions. These styles include Abbasid, Moorish, Fatimid, Byzantine, Ottoman and Persian.

In Qatar, the characteristic type and style of early mosques varied as the region was under different rulers through the Islamic history. The remains of the mosque found in Murwab archaeological site located northwest of Doha show what is considered as the first most primitive mosque layout and model found in Qatar in Abbasid period in the 14th century. Later, during the 16th century, upon military alliance with the Turks, Qatar drove the Portuguese away, and that was the beginning of the rule of the Ottoman Empire over the whole Arabian Peninsula (Amazing Facts, 2010). Even though Ottoman sovereignty was only nominal as the real power and control were in the hands of the sheikhs and princes of local Arab tribes, the Ottoman architecture that was influenced by Byzantine and Persian styles penetrated into the Gulf and had great impact on the architecture of the region. The boom and prosperity of the mosque construction was noticeable in the 18th century, in line with the tribe movements to Qatar land-living due to the wealth of trading, pearl diving, and the spread of Koranic school and Islamic education that were set under the mosque's administration. It was during Sheikh Jassim bin Mohammed bin Thani (1826–1913), the founder of the modern state of Qatar, that the new types of layout and design were introduced in planning and construction of the mosques.

As explained by Dr. Mahmoud Khadrawi in his book about Qatar's mosques *History and Architecture* (2009), the architectural styles of the mosques constructed in Qatar in the period from 9th to 20th century are divided in seven categories that have evolved during different colonization periods and are affected by different style of architecture. The most popular are the Abbasid, Byzantine, Ottoman and Persian styles:

- the first category is the one replicating the model of the early mosque of AlMurwab, where the layout consists of an open courtyard and aisle of *qibla* including single *riwaq*, *mihrab* and *minbar*;
- the second model is the exceptionally impressive type of mosque layout including open courtyard, aisles of *qibla* and four *riwaq* covered by half circular domes. This type was first recorded in AlZubarah in the north of Qatar and was replicated in Doha by the founder of modern Qatar, Sheikh Jassim bin Mohammed bin Thani, in 1878;
- the third category is a type of a mosque, which consists of an open courtyard and aisles of *qibla*, two *riwaq*, *mihrab*, *minbar* and minaret; it is evident in the 19th-century mosque in AlKhuwair;
- the fourth category is a replica of the third category, the difference being the placement of *mihrab*. In this new type of mosque, *mihrab* was placed on the east side opposite to the aisles of *qibla*;
- the fifth model of mosques constructed in Qatar has an open courtyard with aisles of *qibla* of three *riwaq* in addition to other main elements of the mosque;
- the sixth category of the mosque plan consists of a small open courtyard and aisles of *qibla* including the prayer hall covered with a large dome surrounded by a group of smaller domes of equal sizes, as well as other important elements such as the *mihrab*, *minbar*, and the minaret. Grand mosque (*masjid AlShuyoukh*), built in the early 1960s, situated by the *Emiri Diwan* in the city of Doha, is the first example of this architectural type;
- the seventh category includes a number of mosques built in the mid-end of the 20th century with a layout consisting of aisles of *qibla*, multiple corridors, one or even two levels, and other common architectural elements of mosques with the presence of more than one minaret.

10.
Layout of AlThakhira Mosque following the fourth type of layout of the early mosques of Qatar. Khadrawi, 2009

12.
Layout of Grand Mosque of Doha, an example of the sixth type of layout of the early mosques of Qatar. Khadrawi, 2009

11.
Old AKhulaifat Mosque plan following the fifth type of layout of the early mosques of Qatar. Khadrawi, 2009

13.
Layout of Aal Ahmed Mosque of Souk Waqif, an example of the seventh type of layout of the early mosques of Qatar. Khadrawi, 2009

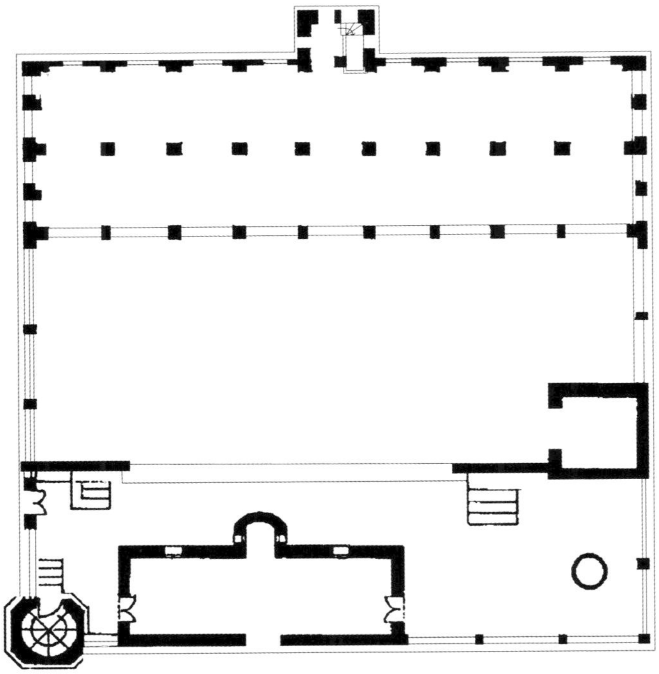

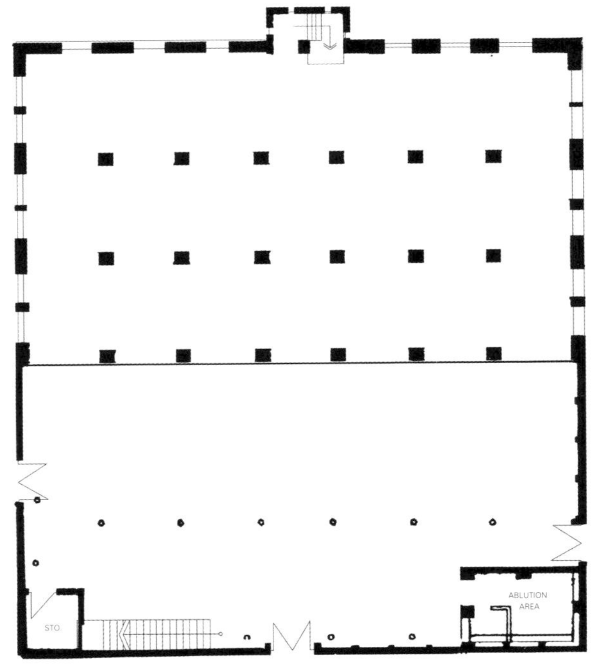

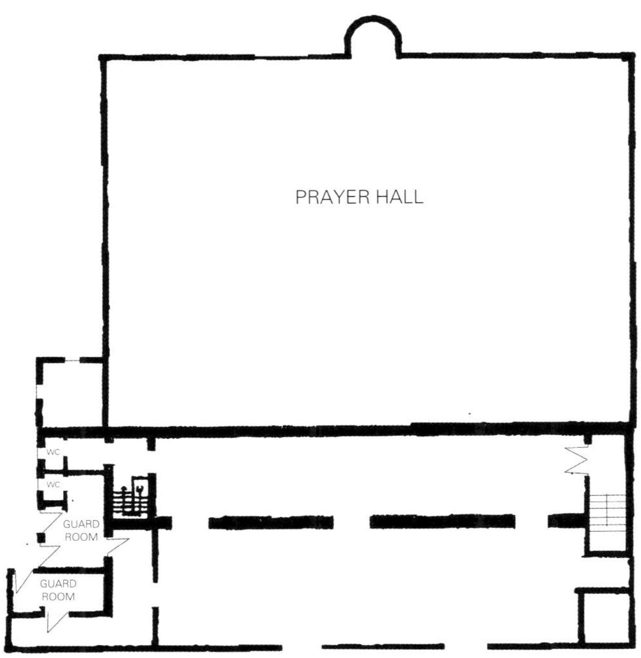

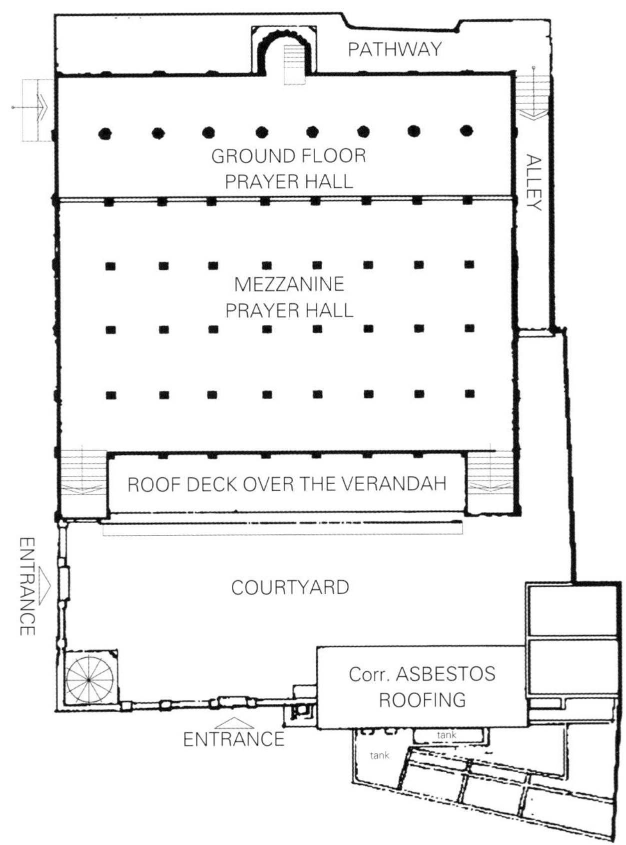

These styles of layout are varied based on numbers of aisles of *qibla* and *riwaq*, however most of mosques in Qatar that have been constructed in 20th century fall into the third category, in which the mosque consists of an open courtyard and aisles of *qibla* with two *riwaq* plus *mihrab*, *minbar* and minaret (Khadrawi, 2009). Significant examples of these type of mosques are presented in the book *The History of Qatari Architecture 1800–1950*.

In the second half of the 20th century, other different types of mosques' layouts were introduced, eliminating the concept of open courtyard with aisle of *qibla*. Most of the mosques around the state of Qatar have been built following this new type and only few old mosques were reconstructed and/or renovated honoring the old layout. One of the most popular upgraded renovated mosques is the AlQubeib mosque, called Sheikh Jassim bin Mohammed mosque, which follows the second model of mosque's layout with covered roof adorned by multiple domes (Khadrawi, 2009).

At the beginning of the 21st century, the state of Qatar begun to gain the reputation of a cultural heart of the Middle East due to the state's focus on knowledge economy as a base for its future development. In line with such a prosperous city development is the state's vision of establishing a vibrant culture of innovation with focus on securing and stabilizing the society through the principles of justice, equality, and the rule of law. Additionally, developing a spirit of tolerance, constructive dialogue and openness towards any nationalities and cultural backgrounds. Thus, during the last decade, there was a tremendous effort by the Ministry of Awqaf to upgrade and construct mosques all over the state, where now in each district more than one mosque could be found. In 2008, the state's ruler, at the time Sheikh Hamad bin Khalifa Al Thani, issued a directive to build a mosque in Doha as Islamic monument and a prominent architectural landmark, positioning Doha at the same level as other prominent Islamic cities known for their historic mosques inherited through generations. The *masjid* was always perceived as a place of worship and as an institution responsible for preserving the Islamic identity. The *masjid*, with its balanced design between traditional and contemporary, is playing the role of a new visual landmark for residents and visitors of Doha. The *masjid* is definitely going to construct a paradigm shift in the architectural and urban narrative of Qatar as it borrows elements from the traditional Qatari and Islamic architectures and creatively introduces design elements previously unseen in mosques in Qatar. In other words, the *masjid* is contributing in the construction of a new unique and distinguished identity of Qatar. The one which respects the past, acknowledges the advance of the present, and aspires for a prosperous future.

Chapter I

Evolution of Multi-domed Mosques

The dome as a three dimensional form was commonly used in spiritual spaces and places. Particularly in mosques, the dome resembles the sky with the symbolic direction towards God. In some cases, the dome's scale, height, ornamentation and openings have created a unique spatial experience. Most of the researchers agreed that the concept of the multi-domed mosque was first introduced in the early Ottoman architecture with the simplest plan, an oblong room covered by a tailed pitched roof internally lined in wood. Soon afterwards all Ottoman mosques were built in the form of a square room covered by stone domes resting directly on the walls; the domed square became the archetype of Ottoman architecture. Different types of mosques evolved by using the domed square in a variety of ways, i.e.:

- the single unit mosque with the prayer hall defined by only one domed square unit;
- the multi-unit mosque with the prayer hall defined by the transversal, longitudinal or both repetitions of the domed square unit;
- Eyvan mosque, derived from Seljuk architecture, where a vaulted or domed space is recessed from a central hall or open courtyard.

At first, square domed mosques were small and simple, but later they very often took on monumental proportions. This went in harmony with the mosque as a building becoming functionally and aesthetically more sophisticated. In the 15th century Ottoman architects began to search for means to create large spaces with as few vertical supports as possible, resulting in the introduction of a new concept of domed mosques. The most famous example of this new architectural concept derives from the architecture of the Seljuk Turks, who controlled Anatolia before the rise of the Ottomans. In this context, multiple domes of equal size are supported by pillars as it is evident in the case of the UluCami mosque, also known as the Great Mosque (Freely, 2011).

Chronological Phases of Multi-domed Mosques in Qatar

A published research about mosques in Qatar shows that the construction of AlQubeib mosque went through three sequential phases. More importantly, its multi-domed design concept was transferred from its origin contex, the north of Qatar, to Doha.

1.1
Riwaq (arcades) of AlMareer multi-domed mosque in AlZubarah before its collapse in 1965.
AlKhulaifi, 2006

1.2
Rows of arcades with protruding pointed arches based on cylindrical pillars that support the domes which roof the aisle of *qibla* in an old mosque in AlZubarah.
AlKhulaifi, 2006

1.3
The old AlQubeib mosque in Doha before it was demolished in 1969.
AlKhulaifi, 2006

End of the 18th Century

The first physical manifestation of multi-domed mosques within the state of Qatar was in line with the construction of the AlMareer fort and AlZubarah surrounding walls in 1740. The mosque was built within the walls of the AlMareer fort, as it was to be at the heart of the community, to serve as a place of worship, education and judiciary court. The master builder of that time introduced the new construction concept imitating the Ottoman multi-domed mosques. Once completed, the mosque was the first one with a multi-domed roof and was named "Jame'e AlMareer".

End of the 19th Century

When Sheikh Jassim bin Mohammed Al Thani visited AlZubarah in 1878, he saw the mosque inside the boundaries of the fort. Impressed by the new multi-domed mosque and its unique visual character, upon his return to Doha he hired a popular master builder named Ibrahim AlHumaili to reproduce the mosque of the AlMareer fort. In the area considered as the heart of Doha settlement, AlHumaili built the replica of the AlMareer mosque. The new mosque was considerably larger in size. The mosque was officially named as Sheikh Mohammed bin Jassim Mosque but among locals it was famously known as "AlQubeib Mosque". Bringing this new construction method to Doha resulted in the development of the new architectural trend and model of planning and designing of mosques in Qatar, characterized by an open courtyard layout with four covered aisles.

Mid-End of the 20th Century

A great number of demolitions, reconstructions and renovations of AlQubeib Mosque is recorded. Due to the extensive deterioration, the mosque was first renovated in the late 1950s. The period of the late 1960s was characterized by the demolition of plenty of historical and traditional buildings in Doha and other Qatari cities. When the modern architectural movement emerged in Doha due to the prosperity resulted from oil revenues, a lot of traditional buildings were demolished in order to be replaced by new and more modern structures. An idea of a modern city was aspired for Doha as a capital city of an emerging Gulf state (Alraouf, 2012). In 1969, AlQubeib mosque was totally demolished and replaced by an ordinary cubical mosque, which was simply a composition of an open courtyard, aisles of *qibla*, two *riwaqs*, *mihrab*, *minbar* and the minaret. Using modern construction materials, such as concrete, which has become available in the Qatari context, AlQubeib mosque was reconstructed in 1980s regaining its initial size and design concept of a multi-domed mosque. In 2006, and with a growing tendency towards preserving and conserving Qatar heritage, the mosque was again renovated using local construction

1.4
The AlQubeib mosque in the center of Doha after the reconstruction in 2012

materials that were commonly used in Qatar in the past such as desert stones – *hasa*, limestone mortar – *juss*, limewash – *nuwra*, earth – *turaab*; which is either comprised of *rawdha* – a cultivatable soil, or sand – *raml*, and mud known as *teen*; and date palm fronds – *sa'af*. Due to the city's massive development in the last decade, the mosque went through another demolishing process in the very beginning of 2009 and it was again reconstructed with the same domed concept and in the same size according to an architectural and urban vision created by the Private Engineering Office, the consulting institution known for its commitment to the heritage of Qatar. The mosque was officially opened for worshipers and visitors on July 2012. Since then, the mosque is not only perceived as a place for performing prayers but it is becoming a destination for scholars, visitors and even tourists coming to see how Qatari architecture was preserved and revived.

The New State Mosque

The economic growth and socio-cultural progress of Qatar in the last couple of decades are solely attributed to the efforts and the vision of His Highness the Father Emir, Sheikh Hamad bin Khalifa Al Thani. The extensive development is balanced in its spiritual intention. The state's vision, also known as Qatar vision 2030, is to establish a multi-faced innovative and stable environment while operating on the principles of justice and equality. By developing a spirit of tolerance, constructive dialogue and openness towards diverse cultural backgrounds, the need for a central large-scale mosque in the city of Doha, the capital of the state, was evident. The mosque was to be a prominent city's architectural landmark, just like in the old Islamic towns. In 2008 a directive to build an iconic state mosque was issued. The emphasis of the mosque design was to be on the preservation of Qatar's national heritage, local identity, and enhanced Islamic values. The mosque was commissioned as a place of worship to preserve the Islamic identity and the spiritual and moral values, realizing the spiritual security of the Muslim nation, reassurance and spread of the good among the faithful.

The project is well distinguished because of its uniqueness, not only in design, but also in planning, which differs from other modern mosques previously built. The Imam Muhammad ibn Abdul Wahhab mosque is considered as one of the most distinctive Qatar projects reflected by its prominence of the perpetual architecture. The use of aesthetic features and patterns from the treasures of Qatari heritage and architecture provides the mosque with a distinguished identity. The construction of the mosque started at the end of 2008 with eminent directives to use exceptionally durable materials in the finishing and

1.5
An axial view of the *masjid*
from the main parking entrance

decorations to suit the character of such a monumental mosque. The mosque's exceptional design provides a balance between authenticity and modernity, expressing the spirit of the age without compromising the value of the past. It took over two years to complete the construction. Once completed the mosque was inaugurated by the Emir H.H. Sheikh Hamad bin Khalifa Al Thani on 14th December 2011.

Naming of the Mosque

The masjid *of Imam Muhammad ibn Abdul Wahhab*

Traditionally, the word mosque or *masjid* is enough to identify the building which is designated for Muslim prayers. Yet according to cultural values, mosques were named after cities or companions of Prophet Muhammad or scholars and Imams. The mosque was initially named as the "State Mosque" since it was visually and symbolically the largest and most dominant mosque in Qatar. Later, before the formal opening, it was officially named the "*masjid* of Sheikh Imam Muhammad ibn Abdul Wahhab." Sheikh Abdul Wahhab was one of the most renowned Muslim theologians, reformer and pioneer of the 18th century Islamic world. As per Qatar National Vision report dated 2011, the decision to name the mosque after the Imam was brought by H.H. Sheikh Hamad bin Khalifa Al Thani. The intention was to revive the nation' symbols and historical icons and maintain its cultural values. It is imperative to note that Sheikh Jassim bin Muhammad Al-Thani, the founder of Qatar (may Allah have mercy upon him), who was both knowledgeable in religion and ruled the state, adopted the message of Sheikh Muhammad ibn Abdul Wahhab and spread it across the state of Qatar and wider in the Muslim world.

Short Biography of Imam Muhammad ibn Abdul Wahhab

While the achievements, teachings and visions of Imam Muhammad ibn Abdul Wahhab are numerous to be mentioned in a short paragraph, it is worthy to highlight the traits of such a leader and intellectual Muslim. Imam Muhammad ibn Abdul Wahhab was a preacher and scholar from Nejd in central Arabia. His full name is Imam Muhammad ibn Abdul Wahhab bin Suleiman bin Ali bin Muhammad bin Ahmad bin Muhammad bin Rashid bin Barid Masyarif bin AlTamimi AlNajdi Hanbali. He was the prominent leader of a religious movement called the Wahhabist. The respected Imam was born in 1703, though some are of the opinion that it was in 1696, which is not widely accepted. He was first educated by his father at Oyayna, a village located at Yamama in Najd, northwest of the city of Riyadh, his homeland. He learned to read the *Qur'an* very early and exerted himself in his studies and advanced learning under the full supervision and guidance of his father, Sheikh Abdul Wahhab bin Suleiman, who was a great jurisprudent and the judge of Oyayna.

In his early adolescence, the Imam went to the Sacred Mosque at Makkah to perform *hajj* and during his visit he seized the opportunity to meet great scholars of Medina. He started his mission calling on people to follow *tawhid* (Oneness of Allah) and the *sunnah* of the Prophet. He announced that it was the duty of every Muslim to follow the Islamic religion strictly in accordance with the *Qur'an* and *sunnah*. Imam Muhammad ibn Abdul Wahhab propagated for removing negative and undesirable innovations in Islam. In his teachings he admonished Muslims to follow only the original values of Islam as typified by the Salaf and to discard exploitations introduced by Bid'ah (heretic innovations). Ibn Abdul Wahhab also studied in Basra in what is now Iraq. By this time he was considered a knowledgeable young scholar, and his teacher, Muhammad AlMujmui, allowed his own children to study with the young Imam. Ibn Abdul Wahhab was motivated above all by the principle of *tawhid* and rejected belief in any idol, and he did not accept that any earthly object could be associated with the divine. Ibn Abdul Wahhab made his way back to the Arabian Peninsula, staying in his hometown and then in AlAhsa, and finally moving to Huraymila, where his father had taken up residence (Martin, 2004). In 1744, Imam Muhammad ibn Abdul Wahhab made an agreement with Muhammad bin Saud that marked the rise of the new Saudi state, Dir-iyah. In Dir-iyah the Imam spent 48 years of his life, filled with writings and preaching. Imam Muhammad ibn Abdul Wahhab died on 20th June 1792 and his body was laid to rest in Dir-iyah (Najd). After the death of the Imam, his sons, grandsons, and followers continued his mission.

1.6
A slant view to the main façade of the *masjid* from the podium level

Chapter II

The Language of Architecture

Urban Geography: Site and Context

The site and the urban context of the mosque are part of the different forces which shaped the design concept, the form and the spatial articulation of the building and its different amenities. The *masjid* of Imam Muhammed ibn Abdul Wahhab is located in the AlJabilat area, in an elevated prime location leading towards the north of the heart of the metropolitan city of Doha. Its eastern and southern façades are overlooking the well-known AlIstiqlal Street; where the famous Qatar Sports Club and AlDana Club can be found; and the vibrant business district of the modern West Bay area. Conversely, the *masjid* is accessible from the west and north via AlKhalifa Street and AlMuhandiseen Street respectively, and is also in close proximity to the residential dwellings of AlDafna area.

The site is physically characterized by the intense heat and the alternating of dryness and humidity, with temperatures reaching 50 °C during summer. Although most of the country is covered by sandy desert planes, the *masjid* site is considered to be more on a low-lying rocky land promoting an axeriscape type of landscape. Around 1642 local desert-grown Sidra trees, shrubs and reeds like phragmites were planted to depict the sceneries. The *masjid*'s internal water network is used to irrigate the green spaces due to the scarcity of rainfall, which is negligible, averaging 100 mm (3.9 in) per year, confined to the winter months, and falling in brief, in addition to the limited underground water mostly with mineral content that is unsuitable for drinking or irrigation; this limits the natural fresh water resources. The probability of being exposed to the sudden and violent dust storms that sometimes descend on the peninsula is quite high due to the location and the plateau type of topography, with slight changes in its elevation. However, the *masjid* orientation toward Ka'aba contributes in maximizing the daylight through the façades openings reducing the need for artificial lighting. Taking into consideration the sun orientation during high summer and deep winter seasons, *masjid* is strategically formed so heat gain and glare are mitigated when sunlight is excessive. The massing of the *masjid* is designed in relevance to sun path as well as wind direction protecting from the dusty North (*shamal*) wind while maximizing the building exposure to the onshore breezes.

Design Concept and Building Form

As previously mentioned, the design concept of the Imam Muhammed ibn Abdul Wahhab *masjid* is derived from the multi-domed building form of the original AlQubeib Mosque, but on a much larger scale. Thus, the *masjid* is imitating the form and style of the mosque that was and until now is considered as one of the most exceptional mosques in the state because of its unique type of layout and exclusive method of construction and roofing the aisle of *qibla* with domes. The layout model is uncommon in Qatar as it derives from the Ottoman architecture. The annexation of new land territories that were ruled by the Ottoman Empire enabled Ottoman architects to promote their design and construction techniques. The concept of multi-domed mosque in Qatar was initially introduced in Jame'e AlMareer mosque at AlMareer fort in Al-Zubarah.

The concept and the form of the *masjid* of Imam Muhammed ibn Abdul Wahhab are derived by combining the so-called "Duplication dome (Rectangular)" and the "Earring (pendentive) dome courtyard" layouts. The overall layout of the mosque relies on the duplication dome layout as it is rectangular in both horizontal and transverse axis. This form of layout is similar to the Islamic architecture of mosques in other regions. The entire plan is divided into spaces by columns or walls. More than one dome can be found in this category, and finding the dominant dome is difficult but not impossible. The spans yielded by the columns and walls used to support the vast area of the roof are surmounted by domes. The domes are arranged in rows and columns in proportion to the dimensions of the plan. The so-called "Earring dome courtyard" layout, which integrates the multiple domes and the courtyard, is also apparent in the Imam Muhammed ibn Abdul Wahhab mosque. The internal plan is similar to multiple dome layouts with an added courtyard of four *riwaq* along the walls roofed by the domes.

The Language of Architecture

The *masjid* of Imam Muhammad ibn Abdul Wahhab is inspired by the image of one of the earliest Qatari historical mosques of ancient time. However with its impressive aesthetic features, modernized style, interesting form, lighting scheme and unique finishing materials, the mosque bridges the gap between past and present and literally aspires to the future. The mosque is located within the context of contemporary Doha. Its formal composition, scale, and façades design help the project to blend

2.1
Duplication dome / rectangular layout. (The domes are arranged in rows and columns in proportion to the dimensions of the plan. Aside from other roofing methods, two semi-domes also flank the dome(s) of the prayer hall)

2.2
Earring (pendentive) dome courtyard layout. (The courtyard has four *riwaq*, i.e. an element in traditional buildings in the form of corridors or galleries along the walls roofed by semi-domes similar to those in the rectangular layout with all possible varieties)

2.3
Combination of two models of Ottoman's domed type of mosques

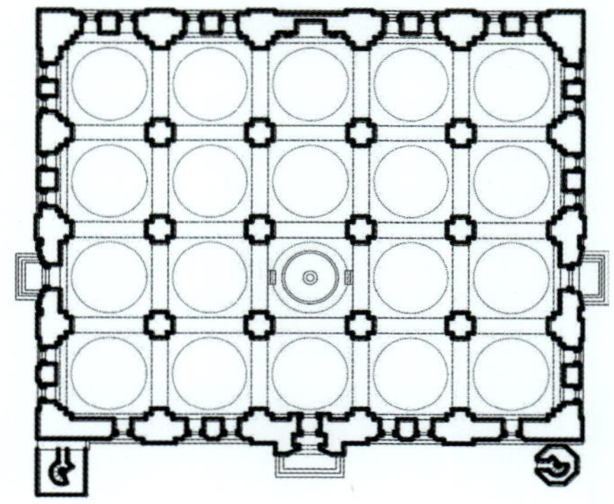

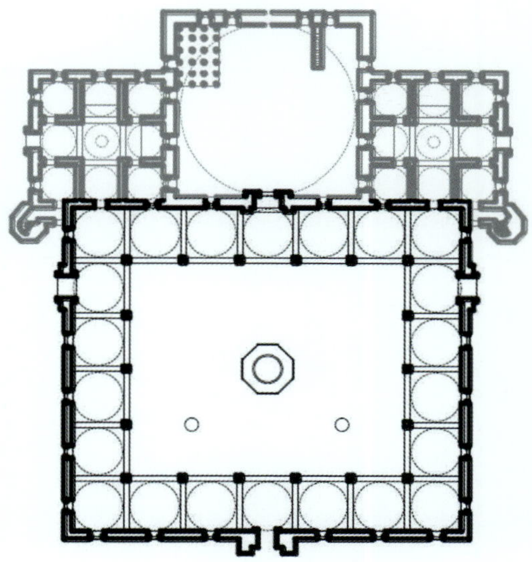

2.4
A model of the mosque of AlQubeib (before its deterioration).
Popular Folklore Magazine: No. 2, April 1986

2.5
Internal view of the old AlQubeib mosque in AlGhanim district showing the row of arcades with protruding pointed arches

harmoniously within the massive urban development of the city. For architects in the Islamic world, the profound challenges are how to balance between tradition and modernity, how to integrate traditional architecture within the contemporary context and how to blend two languages of architecture – traditional and contemporary – and yet end up with a visually, functionally and more important socially and culturally balanced outcome.

Aesthetic Values and Principles

Evaluating the functional aspect of any architectural project is an easy task. For instance, it is relatively easy to determine that the presented design of the *masjid* contains the necessary square footage needed for the prayers or the correct number of rooms needed for the different functions. Yet, when it comes to the complex nature of aesthetics, the debate becomes more difficult and controversial. With its distinctive architectural vocabulary, the design of the *masjid* of Imam Muhammed ibn Abdul Wahhab is visually well manifested and communicated to the users, visitors and even people moving around it. The impact of the mosque is overwhelming as it has a total capacity of 20,678 worshipers. Although the *masjid* was constructed, in its final form, in 2011, the mosque preserves artistically most of the traditional aspects of the region's artistic values. For the user or the visitor of the mosque, an interesting encounter with such history is manifested in unique geometrical patterns, the Arabic calligraphy, the arabesque carvings in wood and iron, as well as the adorned domed ceilings, the floors, the corridors, the hallways and the doors. In other words, every single component of this huge composition is an echo of an artistic value which was documented both in traditional Islamic architecture and in local Gulf architecture as well.

Style and Form

The selected form and style of the mosque are delivering a message of simplicity and humbleness. The *masjid* has been built in a traditional style; its significantly large scale prompts the observer to acknowledge his relative position in comparison with the surrounding built environment. Simple in its form, the building sits on an elevated plateau of a large dimension that compliments its scale positioned and situated in a way that orients the visitors in perceiving, conceiving and using the space. The *masjid* is a highly visible structure, therefore, it has the ability to significantly aid the observer in navigation through the city's built environment. It definitely acts as a landmark in the visual and mental map of Doha. Like other traditional mosques, the orientation and legibility of schemata of the *masjid* of Imam Muhammed ibn Abdul Wahhab are with no doubt articulated with the vertical structure, the minaret, as well as the 99 domes. Emphasizing the aisles of *qibla* as well as giving a clear indication and a gestural

2.6
The site development plan

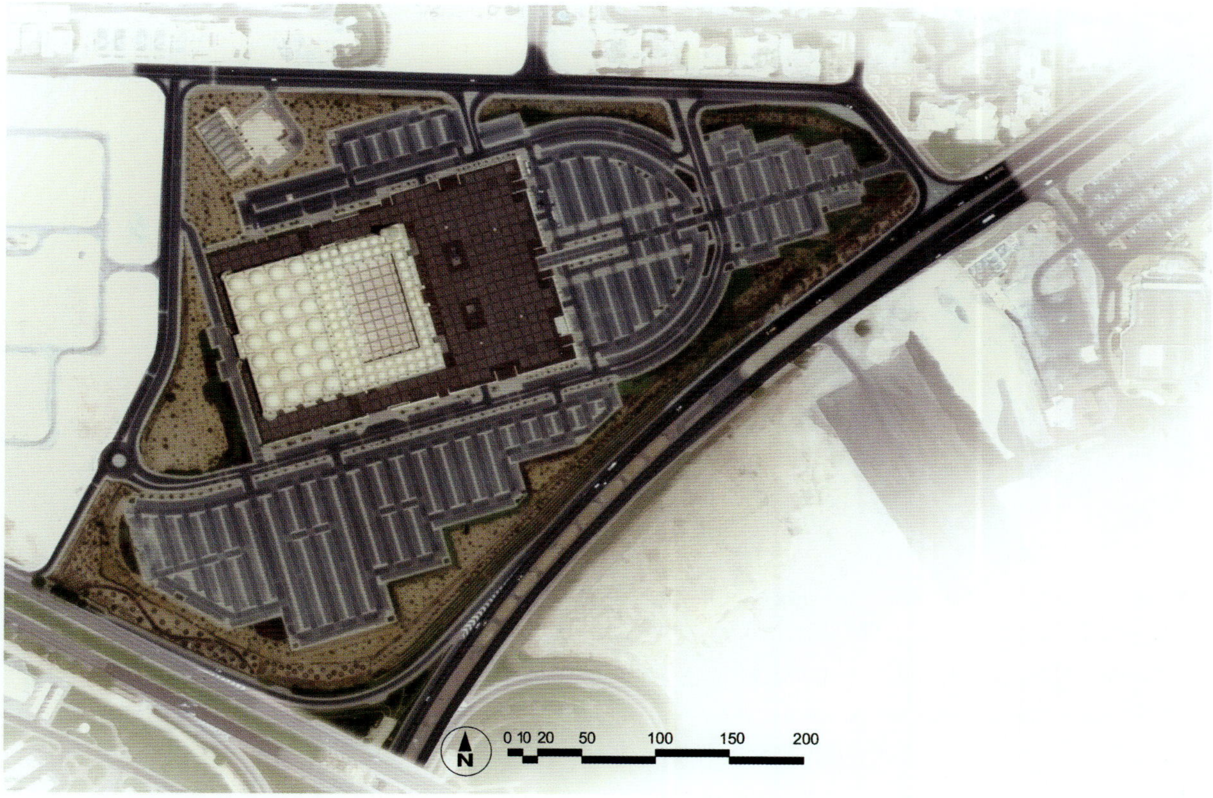

sign of the main entry, the gate of the *masjid* represents a mediator between the inner and outer space. It is a cue of orientation, which sequences the elements of inner spaces.

In the art of architecture, mass, shape, scale, dimension and proportion define the form of the building. The solid mass of the *masjid*, large in the volume and weight, is relative to its surroundings. The shape of the *masjid* is composed of the complex dense surface planes that are well distinguished and remarked by all visitors and follows the form of the middle-eastern type of mosque with square or rectangular plan, known as Arab plan, with domed roof of the prayer hall supported by rows of columns manifesting the hypostyle architecture. Due to the hot climate and the large number of worshipers during Friday prayers, this hypostyle *masjid* has outer arcades surrounding the open courtyard allowing the prayers to enjoy the shade while performing their prayers.

2.7
The dominant position of the mosque
on an elevated plateau

2.8
A view to the mosque from
Khalifa flyover

2.9
A view of the western façade of the mosque showing the landscape and the outside parking lots

2.10
A view to the northern façade of the *masjid* showing the landscape and the outside parking lots

2.11
The general floor plans of the *masjid*

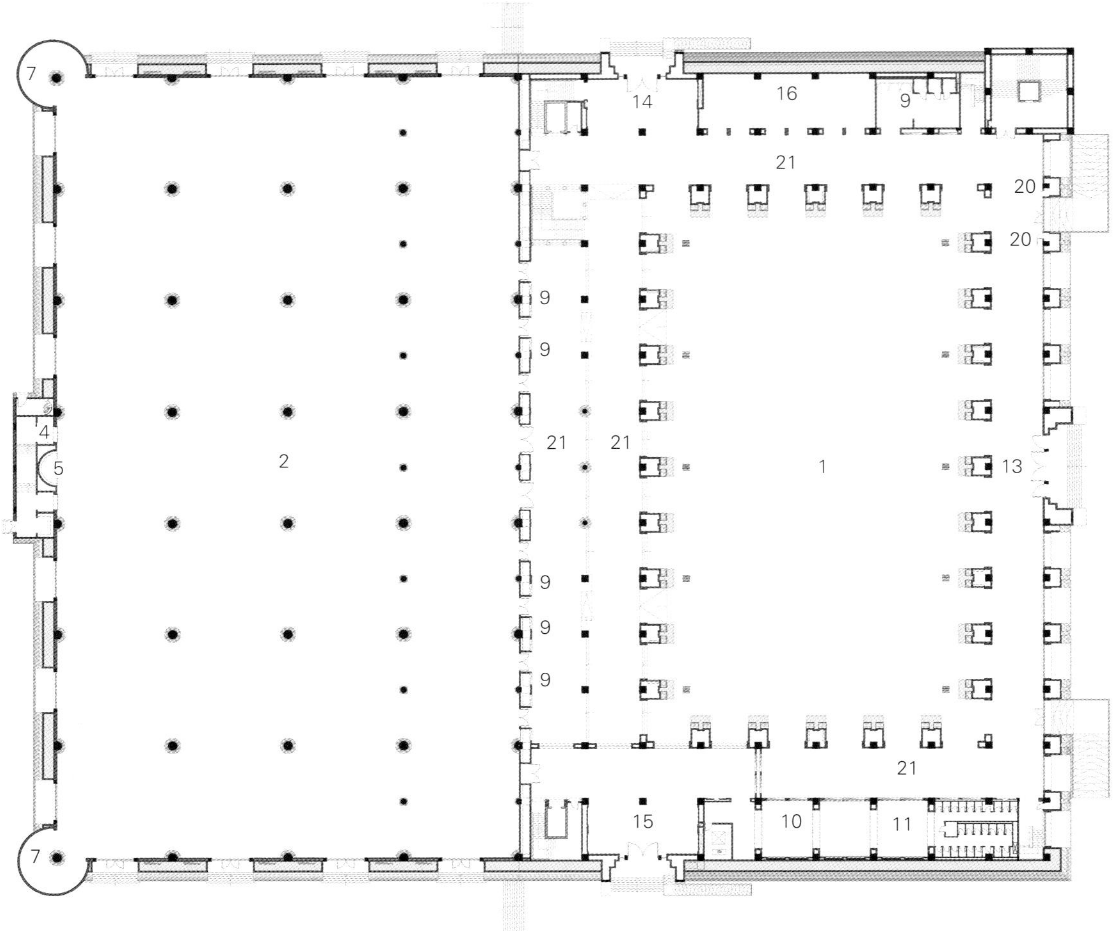

Ground Floor Plan

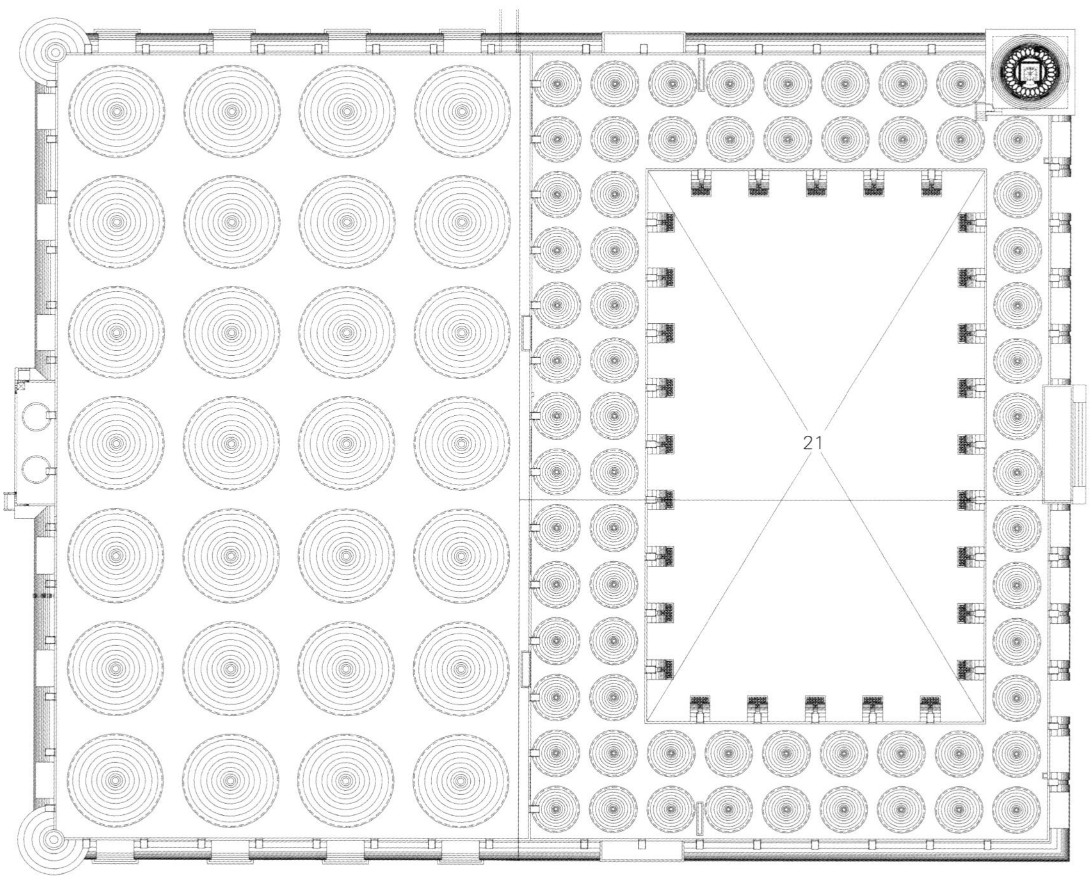

Roof Floor Plan

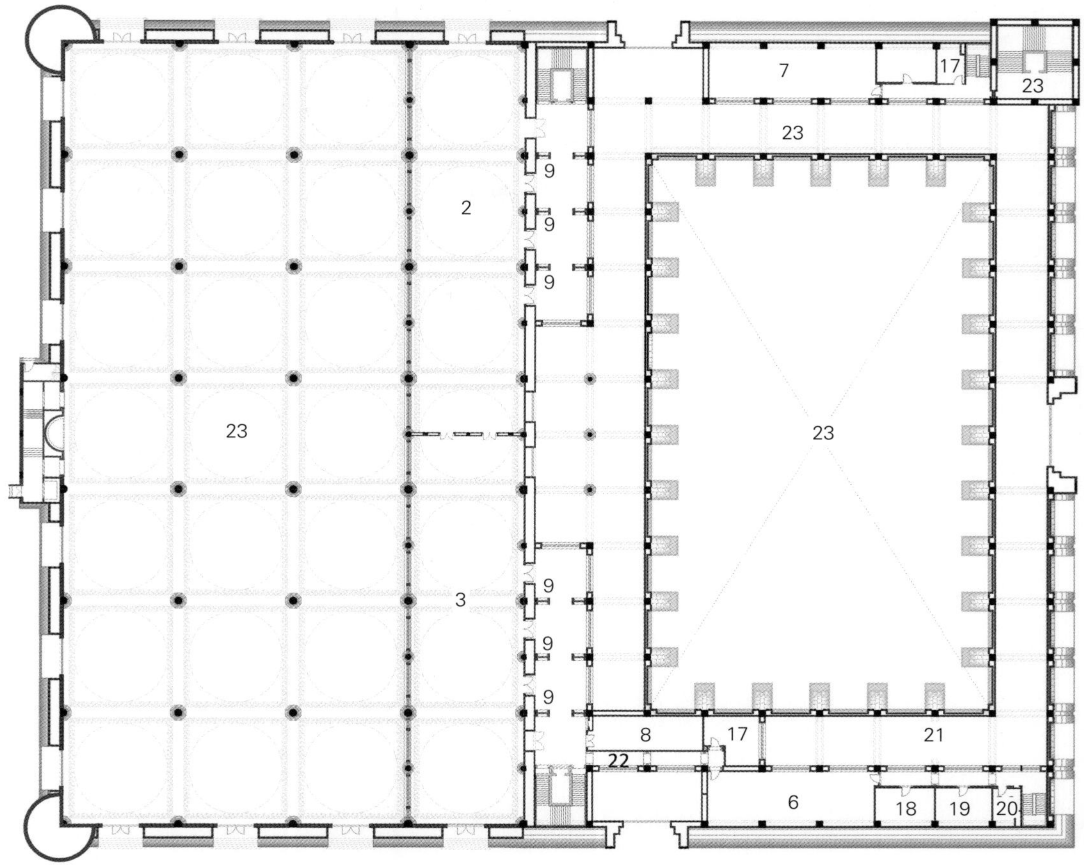

Mezzanine Floor Plan

Legend

1. Open Courtyard
2. Prayer Hall
3. Ladies' Prayer Hall
4. *Minbar*
5. *Mihrab*
6. Library
7. Reading Corner
8. Qur'an Memorizing Center
9. Disabled Ablution
10. Ladies Ablution
11. Toilet and Wash
12. Central Shoe Rack
13. Main Entrance Lobby
14. Secondary Entrance Lobby
15. Ladies' Entrance Lobby
16. Shoe Rack
17. Administration
18. TV Room
19. Security Room
20. Services
21. Corridor
22. Passage
23. Void (Open Courtyard)

2.12
East – the front façade of the *masjid*

2.13
North – the side façade of the *masjid*

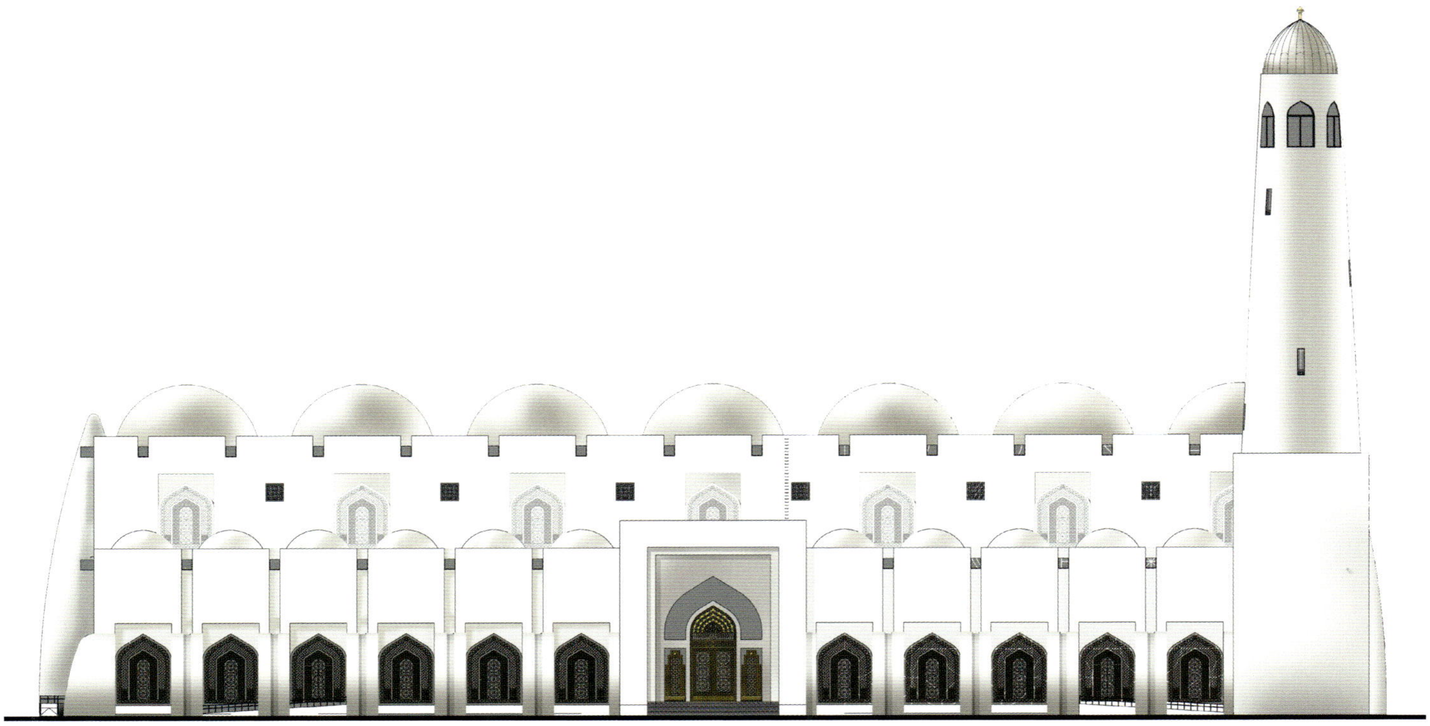

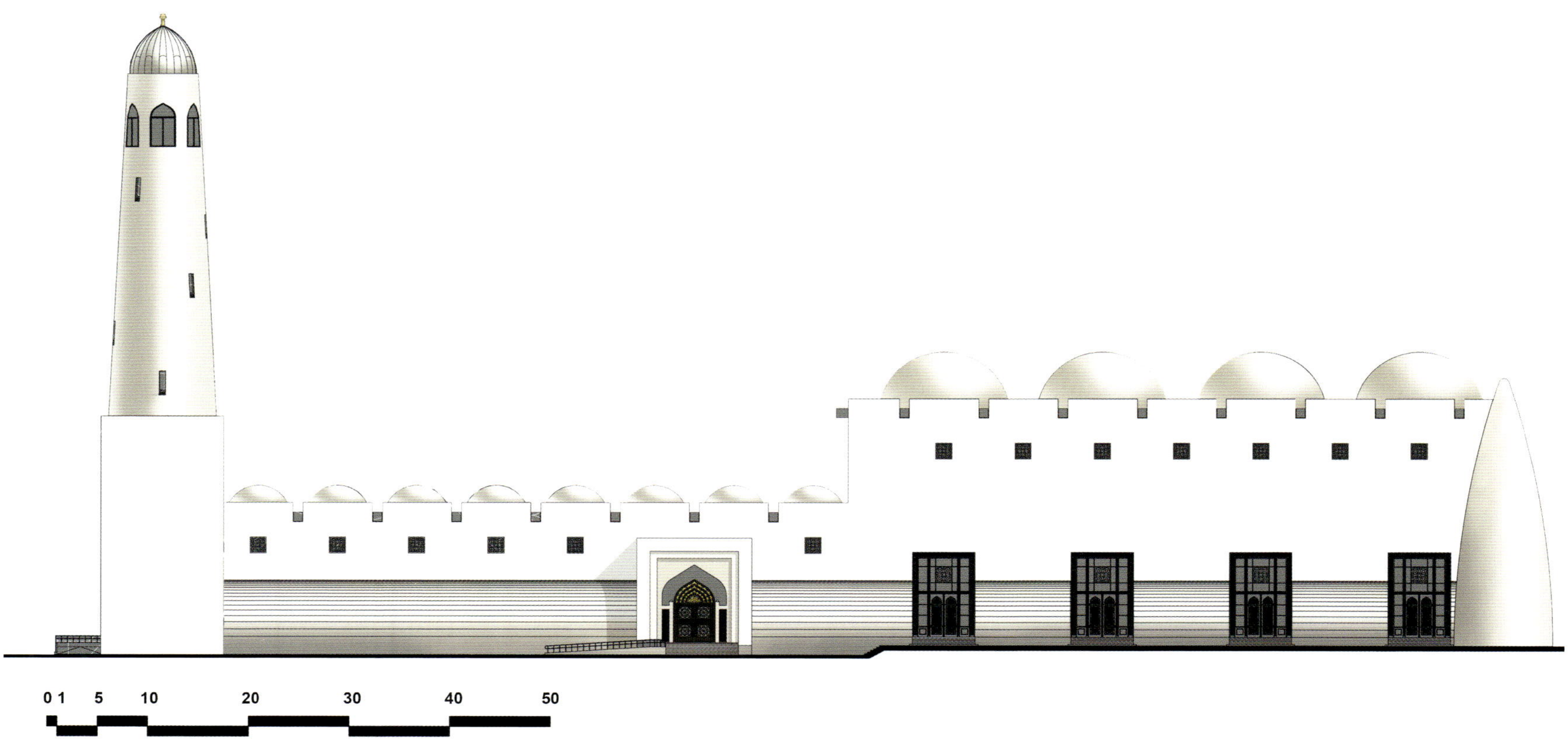

2.14
West – the rear façade of the *masjid*

2.15
South – the side façade of the *masjid*

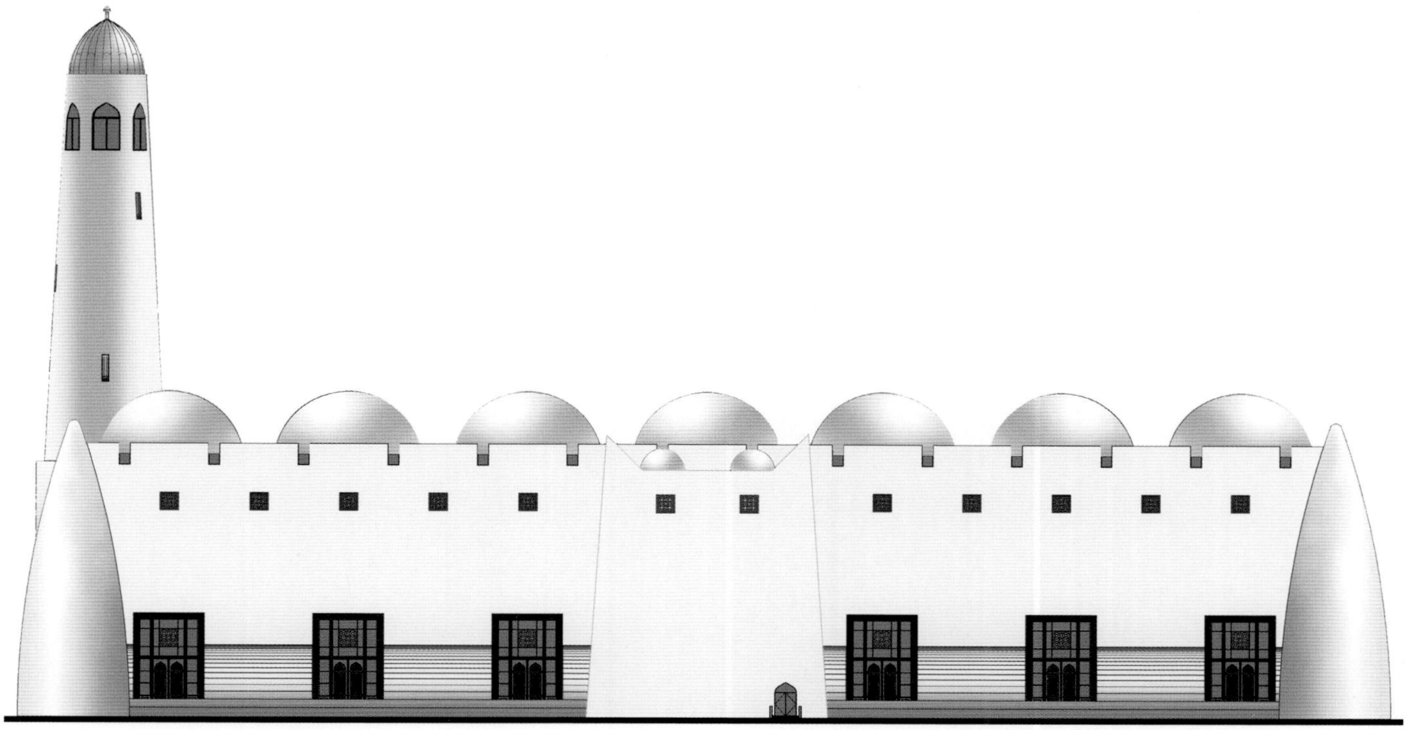

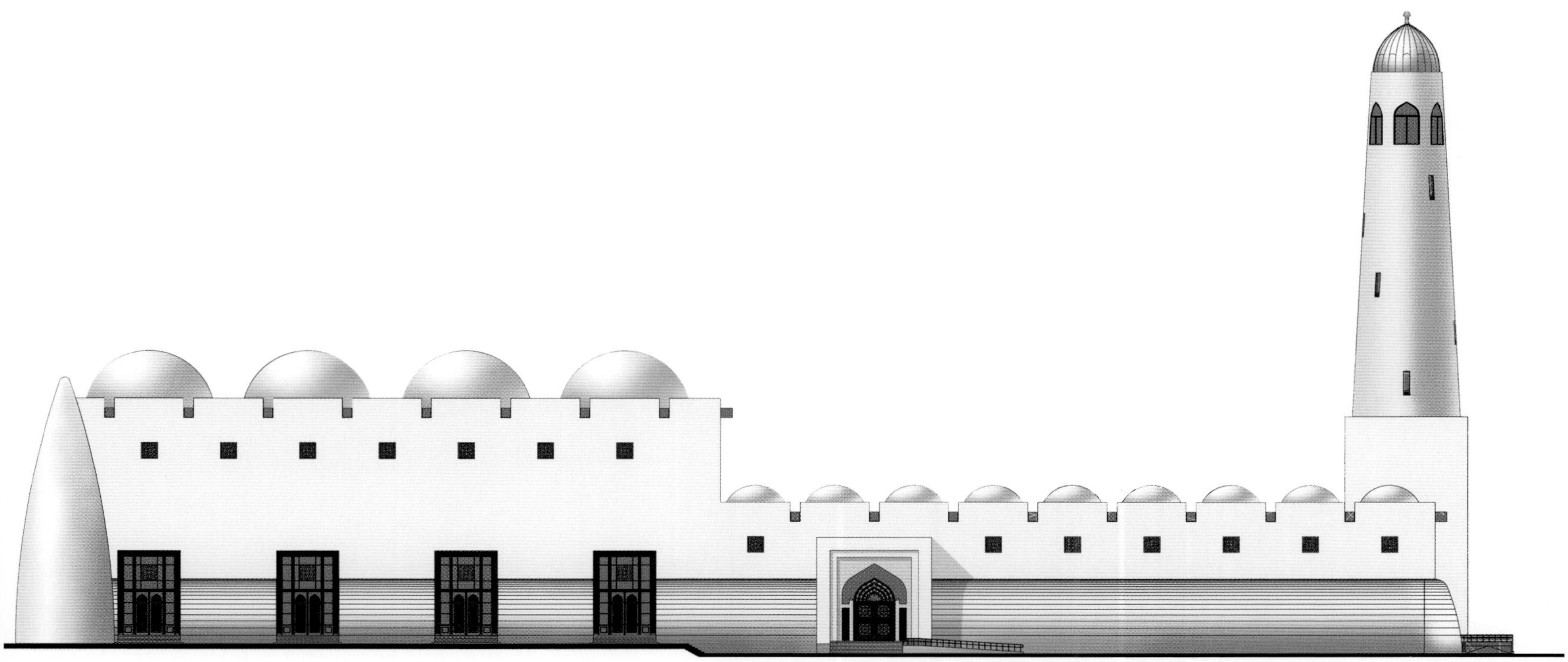

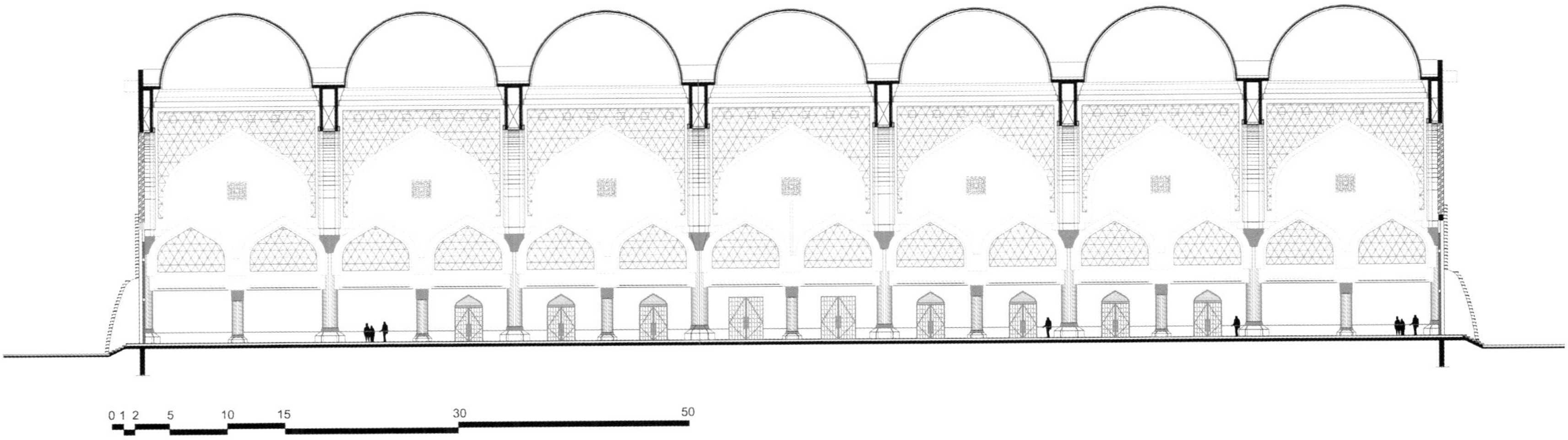

2.16
Transverse section of the *masjid* illustrating the inner area of the *riwaq*

2.17
Longitudinal section of the *masjid* portraying the inner area of the courtyard and the prayer hall

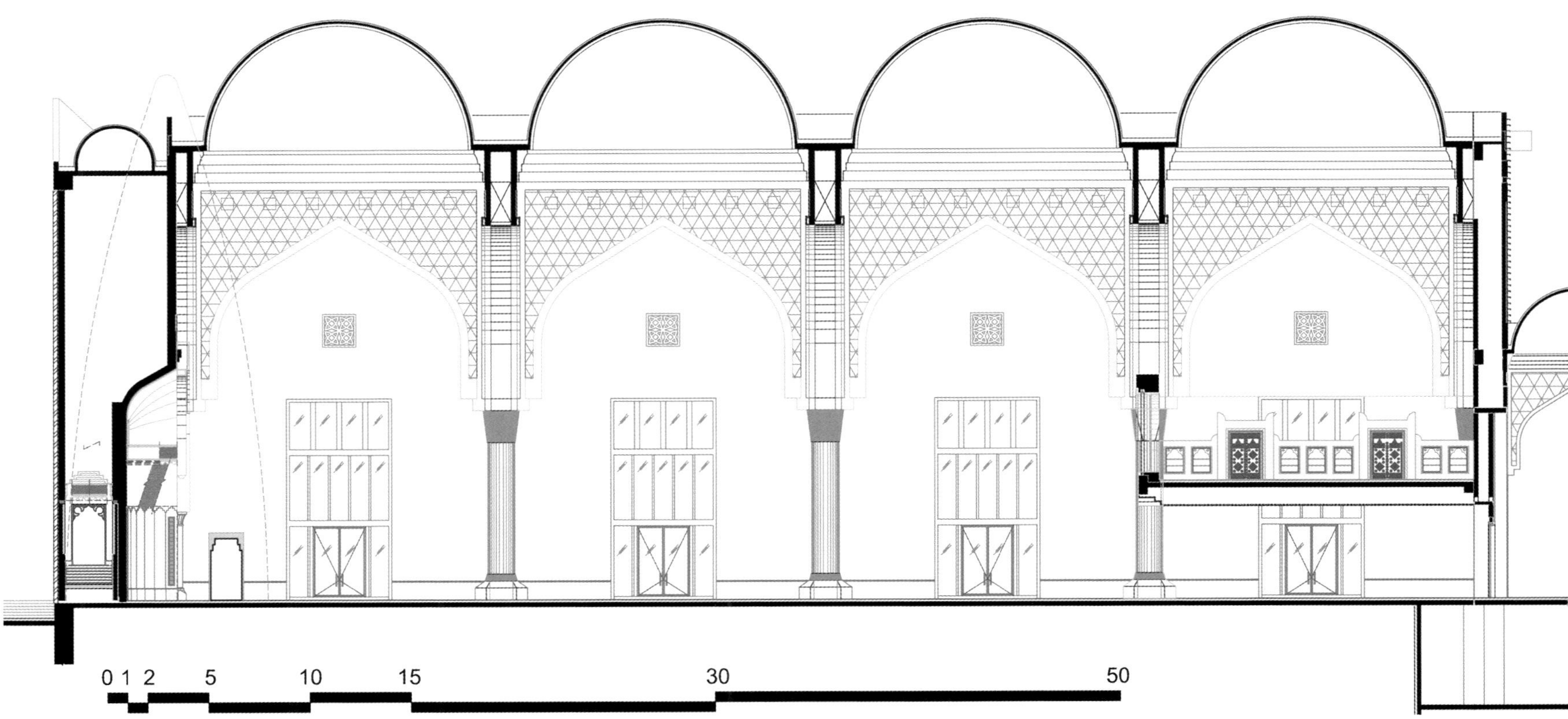

2.18
Transverse section of the *masjid* illustrating the inner area of the *musalla*

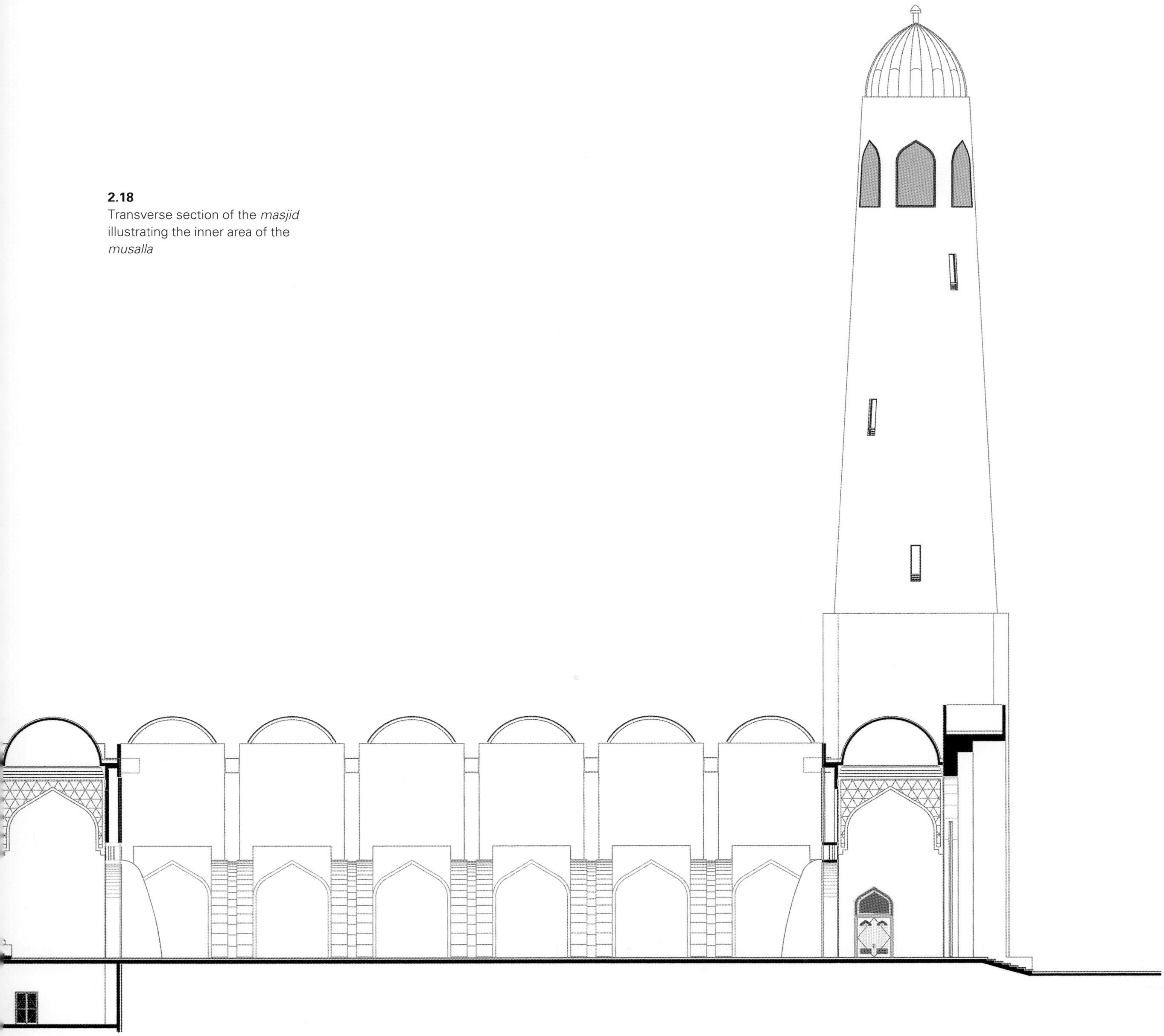

2.19
A view to the main entrance
of the mosque with the parking lots

2.20
A view to the eastern outside parking lots of the *masjid*

2.21
A north-eastern view of the mosque from the podium level

Lighting

A lot of architects and interior designers agree upon the vital importance of lighting in mosques. Lighting scheme in a mosque if successful might enhance the spiritual experience and encourage prayers to have a more profound contemplation and concentration on their prayers. In the case of *masjid* Imam Muhammed ibn Abdul Wahhab, around 157 circular multi-layered brass chandeliers of different size are hanged on the rise of 14 meters, used to lit and adorn the prayer hall, corridors and hallways. The largest chandelier is raised up to 7 meters from its base to the suspension point. The lighting is controlled through automatic system commensurate with the amount of sunlight within different times of the day; accordingly artificial lighting is maximized when the amount of natural light entering the prayer hall through the openings is minimal. The lights of the *masjid* have maintained a tradition of changing color when celebrating different religious occasions throughout the year such as Eids and Ramadan. The external car parking lights up at night by 1816 short stone light poles that were specially manufactured to fit the pavement basalt stone material. Additionally, 120 specially designed stone terraces containing lighting equipment are spread all around to light up the outer yard, along with the traditionally designed lamps on the edge of the walls. The *masjid* looks histrionic, dramatic and impressively lit at night using the intelligent lighting system designed to portray the architectural and aesthetic value of the *masjid* thanks to the hidden lighting system, the indirect lighting, and the LED. The new BAS (Building Automation System) is integrated to adjust and monitor air conditioning, firefighting, sound, lighting and broadcasting systems.

2.22
The bottom view of a round brass-chandelier hanged from the domed ceiling of the *riwaq*

2.23
A string of single-layered chandeliers suspended from the center of domes roofing the *riwaq*

2.24
A close-up of the double-layered brass chandelier suspended from the domed ceiling of the *riwaq*

2.25
Decorative brass hanging points of chandelier holding brass sticks inlaid by perforated brass ball

2.26
Multi-branch suspension sticks and chandelier hanging-point

2.27
Single brass stick and modest chandelier hanging-point

2.28
Section of the *riwaq* chandelier showing decorative brass and lighting bulb

2.29
The double-layered brass chandeliers in the prayer hall of the *masjid*

2.30
An angle view to the succession of suspended single-layered chandeliers

2.31
A closer view of a hanging brass-chandelier in the prayer hall

2.32
The bottom view of a round hanging brass-chandelier in the prayer hall

2.33
A single-layered brass-chandelier in the library

2.34
A single-layered chandelier with central colored glazed base

2.35
Decorative brass wall lantern fixed to the marble and mosaic cladded column

2.36
Profile view of the brass wall lanterns

2.37
The colored glass base bottom of the cylindrical brass wall light

2.38
The half-cylindrical wall lanterns fixed on the staircase walls

2.39
A touching scene of colors changing on the *masjid*'s façade turning to blue and pink during the Muslim's occasions of Ramadan and Hajj

لبيك اللهم لبيك لبيك لاشريك لك لبيك
ان الحمد والنعمة لك والملك لاشريك لك

2.40
A dramatic night shot of north-eastern façade of the *masjid*

2.41
Nocturnal view to the *masjid* from the podium level

2.42
Spot and direct lanterns and short-pole lamps on the buttresses

2.43
Night perspective of the *masjid* from the parking lots to the northern façade

2.44
The cove lights illuminating the arches and the spotlights enlightening the wooden gargoyles stretched out of the façade walls

2.45
The spotlights vivifying the mottled GRC screen grooved into the outer walls of the façades

2.46
Light poles used to light the landscape areas in the northern and western sides of the *masjid* podium level

2.47
Custom-made lamps fixed on the edge of the external wall surrounding the podium level

2.48
Cove lights used to light the red marble of the stairways

2.49
Marble stone terrace boxes with brass frame equipped with lights to lit the podium level of the *masjid*

2.50
A close view to the marble stone light boxes fixed on top of the granite tiles of *masjid*'s podium level

Materials

The building materials used for both the exterior and interior of the *masjid*, were selected based on their appropriateness for the building type, durability, impact on the environment, climatic conditions, and the prevailing architectural design and character of the materials installation, with a major focus on getting final luxurious finishing that holds the individual parts and components of the *masjid* complex all together. Multicolored granite tiles with a special order shaping geometric pattern are used for the floor finishing of outdoor corridors, the *riwaq*, and the courtyard, while mottled marble tiles are used as a fashion-forward flooring choice for inner hallways, entrance lounges and corridors, as well as ablution and wet areas. Additionally, white marbles are used to cover the pillars within the prayer hall with small brass doors located in the northern ribs of the column's crowns. A 7,040 square meters carpet made from natural wool with a simple and elegant design is used in the floor finishing of the prayer hall, library and reading areas. Though, the *masjid* has been built using new materials, but then again the final exterior finishing has been rendered using a fine-tuning of sandstone expressing and manifesting the same image of old AlQubeib Mosque. Both the open parking and internal streets are paved using natural basalt stone, which gives a higher aesthetic value in comparison to the asphalt.

2.51
Simple and mottled granite tiles of podium level with marble balustrade surrounding the outside escalators

2.52
Exterior marble finishing stairs connecting the parking lots to the podium level

2.53
Close-up of mottled marble tiles used in carpeting of the *riwaq*

2.54
Mottled marble tiles used in carpeting of the *riwaq*

2.55
Masala's carpet made from natural wool with simple patterned lines indicting rows of prayer

2.56
Marble cladded columns with brass mottled perforated belt

2.57
Natural basalt stone with which open parking and internal streets are paved

2.58
Sandstone exterior finishing

2.59
Sandstone exterior finishing with projected wooden gargoyle

Statistics and Technical Aspects of the Mosque

The technical drawings best show the unique layout of the simple mosque replicated on a much larger scale. The drawings illustrate the simplified elevations of the architectural language used. The total plot size of the *masjid* of Imam Muhammad ibn Abdul Wahhab is about 175,575 square meters including the *masjid*, the park, the shaded and open car parking, as well as some utility buildings:

- the total covered area of the *masjid* is 19,565 square meters encompassing the courtyard and the prayer hall;
- the *masjid* is surrounded by a green belt enfolding the outside car parking with a total area of 47,362 square meters containing a combination of seasonal plants, flowers and various shrubs, and trees;
- an open parking and internal streets spread over an area of more than 80,000 square meters and can accommodate up to 2,615 cars. However, the shaded parking within the basement level with a total area of 14,470 square meters has a capacity of 350 cars. This brings the total number of car parking slots to 2,960. The basement car parking is connected to the open ground-level parking through two separated entrances and exits, while the basement level is linked to the ground level by two electric escalators and stairs surrounding the outer yard.
- utility buildings include electrical sub-stations, standby generators, HVAC, firefighting, irrigation system and pumping, as well as operation and maintenance offices, covering a total build-up area of 2,414 square meters. These services are connected to the *masjid* via an underground tunnel and reach to the air-handling units in the basement.

Chapter III

Poetics of Architecture: Elements of the Masjid

Throughout the history of the Islamic nation, mosque were multi-functional places. Yet, in the contemporary times, there is a tendency to transform the mosque into a place for only performing prayers. The case is different at Imam *masjid* as both the client and the architect believe in the vitality of the mosque and its multi layered role. Besides being used for prayers, mosques are also used for study, or simply as a place for contemplation and reflection. The main mosque of a city, used for the Friday communal prayer, is called a *jumaa masjid* (literally translated "Friday mosque"). The style, layout and decoration of a mosque tell us a lot about Islam in general, but also about the period and region in which the *masjid* was constructed. Although prayers can be performed privately, either indoors or outdoors, nearly every community of Muslims dedicates a space or building for congregational prayer. Each community in different cultures will add to the roles and the functions of the mosque to make it authentically the heart of the city or town. Therefore, the images of the mosques around the world reveal that there are impressive variations derived from climatic, economical, cultural and social factors.

Design features and building materials greatly vary and are directly influenced by the culture, heritage and resources of each local Muslim community. Yet, there are some features that nearly all mosques have in common. The parts of a mosque are practical, and provide both continuity and a sense of tradition among Muslims worldwide. The architecture of a mosque is shaped most strongly by the regional traditions of the time and place where it was built. As a result, style, layout and decoration can vary greatly. Nevertheless, because of the common function of the mosque as a place of congregational prayer, certain architectural features appear in mosques all over the world.

The morphological components and elements of Imam Muhammad ibn Abdul Wahhab *masjid* complex are the prayer hall (*musalla* or *haram*) for both male and female prayers; the niche (*mihrab* or *maqsarah*) indicating the direction of *qibla*; the raised platform (*minbar*) attached to the *mihrab* and allocated for Imam to give speech; the tower for prayers calling (the minaret), a cylindrically shaped vertical element raised upon square base; the ablution area, and a facility designed for ritual purification (*wudu'*). More essential components include the courtyard and socio-cultural area (*sahn*); an open area adjoined to the prayer hall containing fountains with potable water; and aisles of *qibla* (*riwaq*) parallel to the *qibla*. In addition, one significant component of the mosque are the external drinking fountains (*sabeel*)

3.1
An axial view of the *musalla* from the main male entrance toward the *mihrab*

3.2
A view to the northern inner façade of the *musalla*

3.3
A view of the eastern inner façade of the ground floor *musalla*; also seen is the mezzanine prayer hall

3.4
The south-eastern view of the ground floor *musalla* interior; also seen is the mezzanine prayer hall

3.5
The base of the pillar in the prayer hall holding copies of holy *Qur'an*

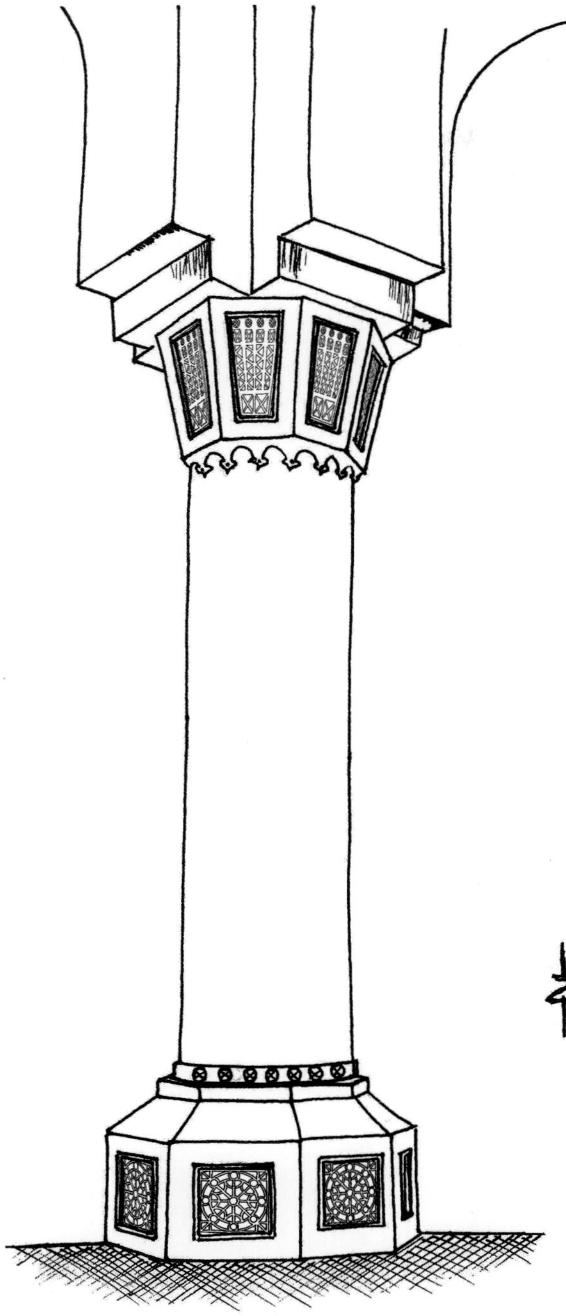

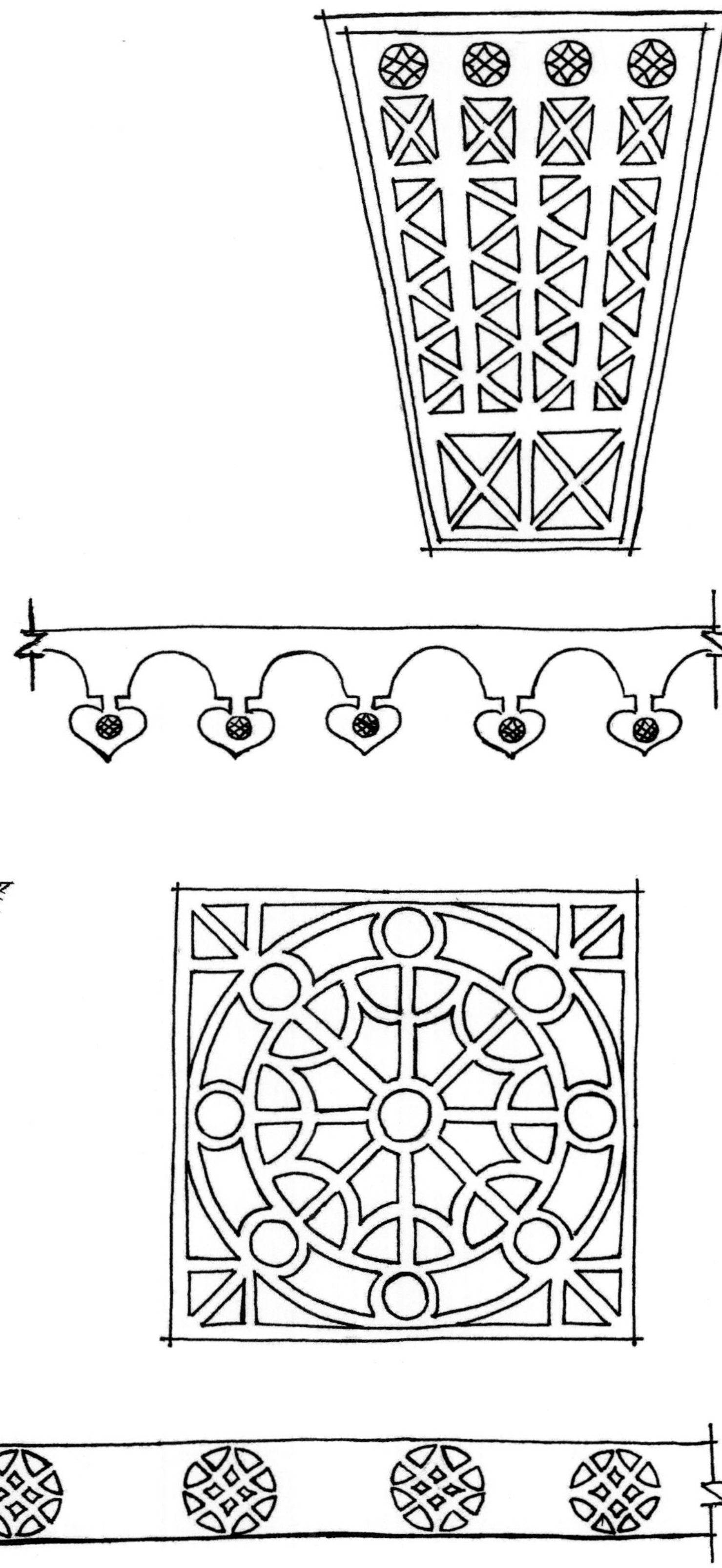

3.6
Central clock system at *mihrab* area

3.7
A transverse section of the mosque showing the inner space of the *musalla*

3.8
Typical border detail at prayer hall

3.9
Door frame at reading corner within prayer hall

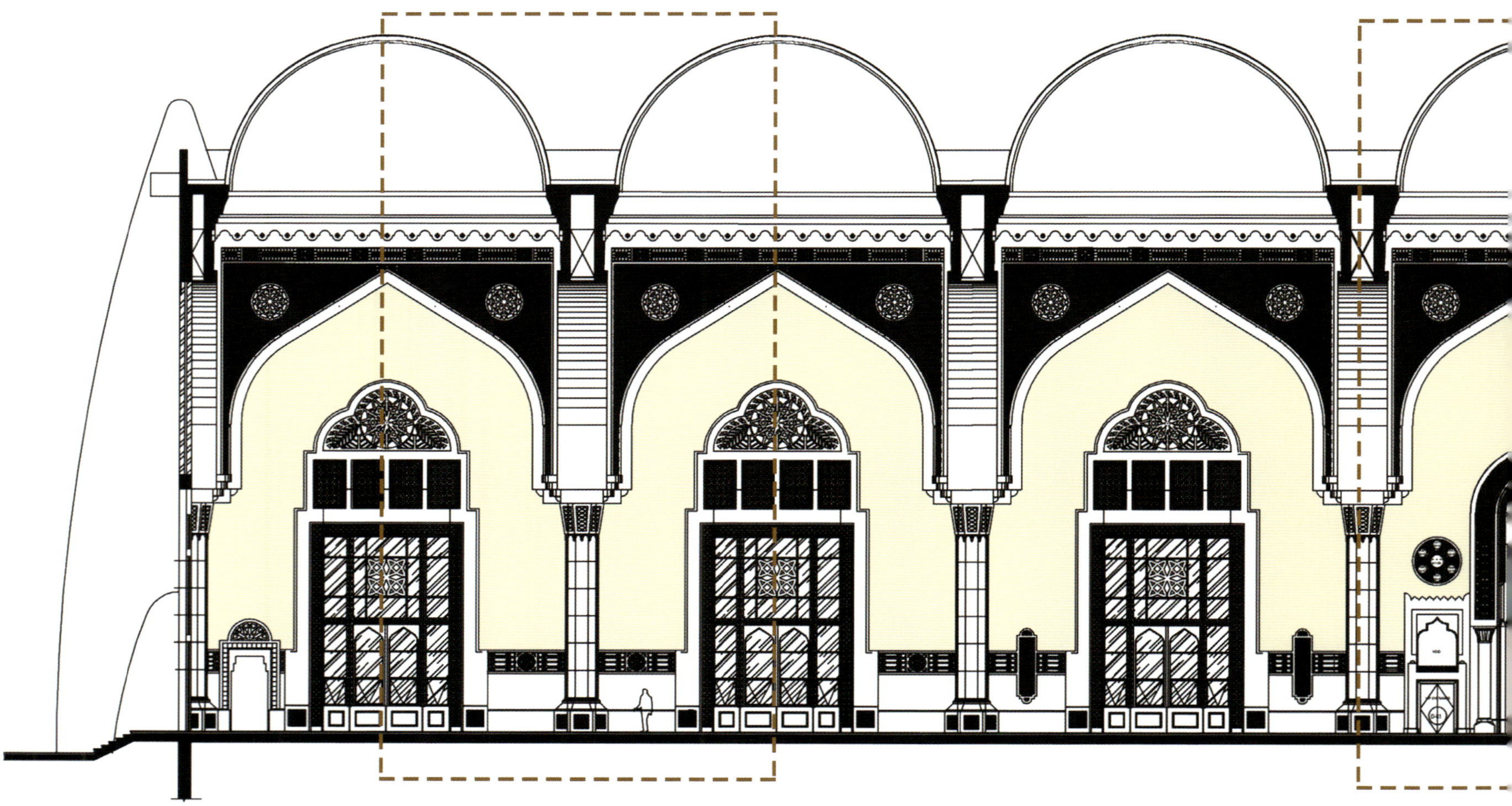

3.10
The bookshelves placed along the screens of the mezzanine floor prayer hall

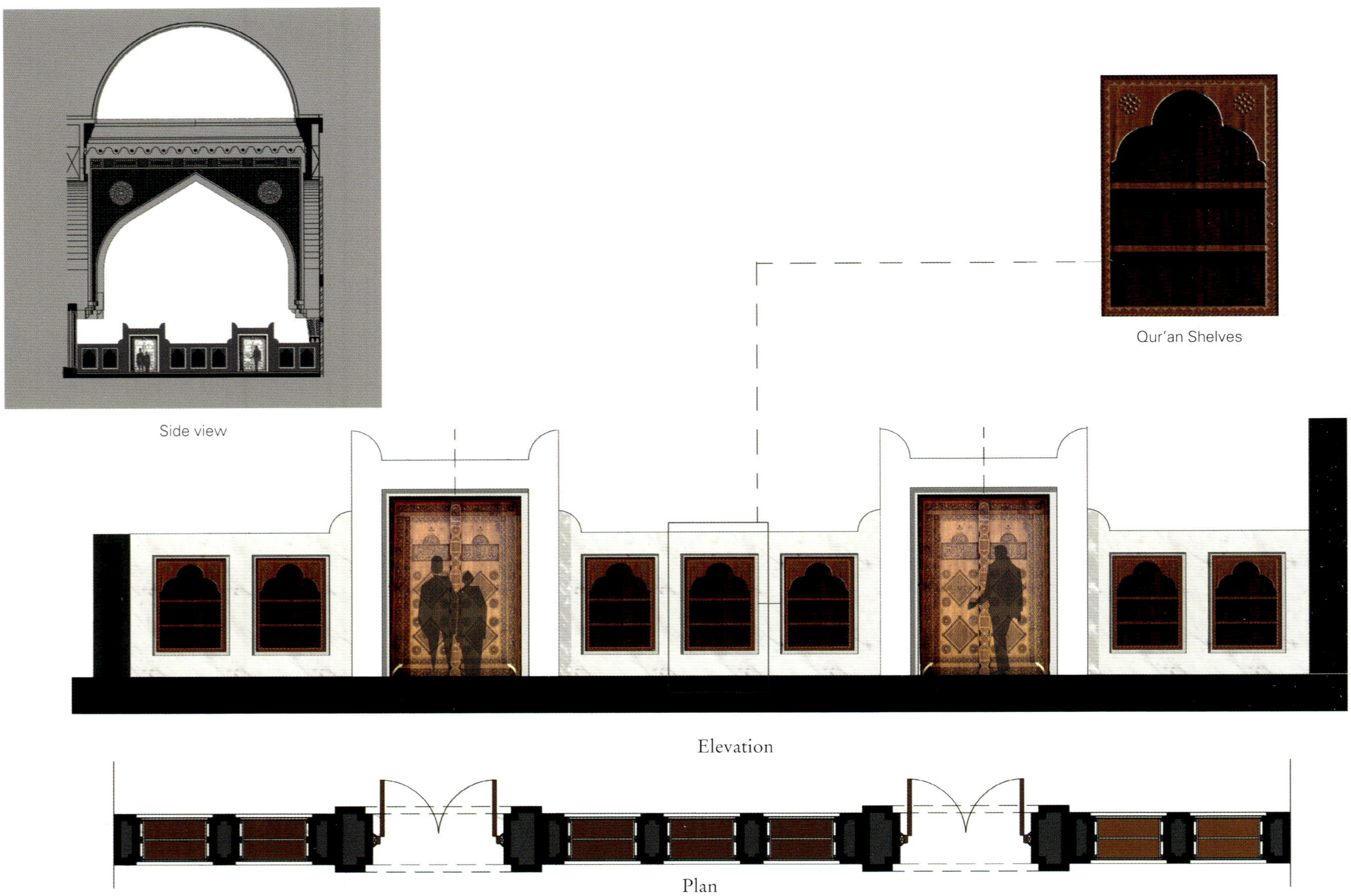

3.11
A design drawing showing the shoe racks beside the inner entrances of the prayer hall area

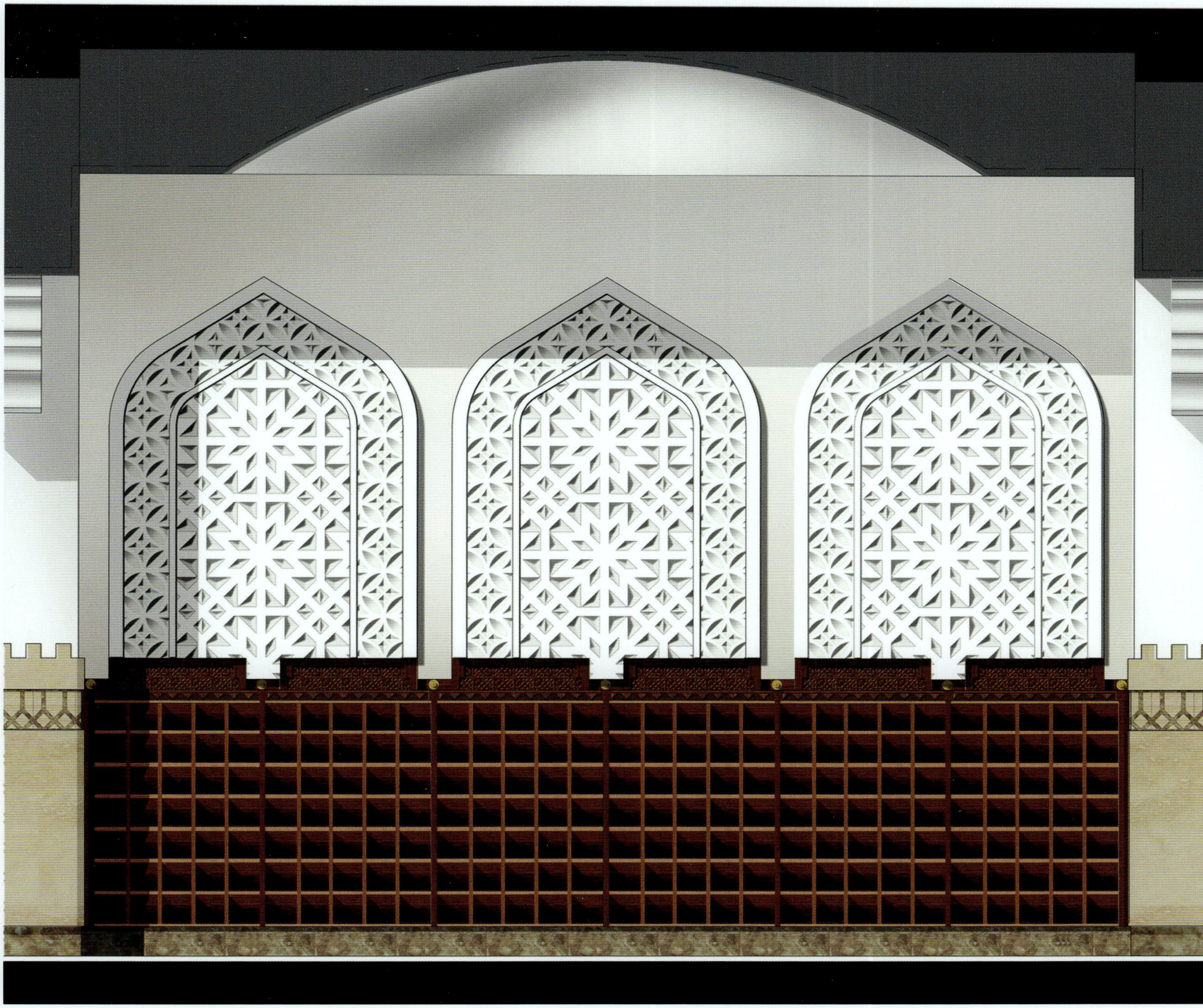

3.12
View from the southern outdoor corridor (*riwaq*) toward the north-eastern side of the courtyard where the minaret is placed

surrounded by four sides of square plan buttress with domical roof. In the following paragraphs, more details about these essential elements are described.

Musalla

The central area for prayer is called a *musalla* or *haram* (literally, "place for prayer"). The prayer hall of Imam Muhammad ibn Abdul Wahhab *masjid* is deliberately quite bare, as no furniture is required, since worshipers sit, kneel and bow directly on the floor that is covered with a simple red carpet made of natural wool. There are few chairs or benches to assist elderly or disabled worshipers who have difficulty with mobility. Along the walls and within the base of pillars in the prayer hall, are bookshelves to hold copies of the *Qur'an*, wooden book stands (*rihal*), other religious reading material, and individual prayer rugs. The prayer hall accommodates precisely 9,990 worshipers, in the ground floor. However, the mezzanine prayer hall accommodates additional 2,400 worshipers divided in two sections for male and female with equal capacity of 1,200 worshipers for each section, bringing the total capacity to 12,390.

Sahn

A *sahn* is a courtyard in Islamic architecture. Imam Muhammad ibn Abdul Wahhab *masjid* has a large central *sahn*, which is considered to be an open central courtyard that accommodates up to almost 8,332 worshipers. Like other mosques' courtyards, the water features are present in the *sahn* of the Imam Muhammad ibn Abdul Wahhab *masjid.* These are small potable water fountains embedded into the buttresses structurally holding the arcades surrounding the courtyard. The courtyard is mainly accessed through an iron gateway that differs in design from other doors and holds a great architectural and symbolic value.

Riwaq

Riwaq or an arcade is considered as one of the most prominent Islamic architectural elements that often surround and define the courtyards of mosques (*sahn*). It is traditionally a place for meeting,

3.13
A view to the center of the *sahn* toward the minaret of the *masjid* and the northern arcade

3.14
Brass screens enclosing the *sahn* of the *masjid*

3.15
Axial night view to the *riwaq* surrounding the courtyard

3.16
A view to the north-west corner of the *sahn*

3.17
Drinking fountains embedded into the buttresses facing the *sahn*

3.18
A detailed hand-sketch showing the installation details of the drinking fountain

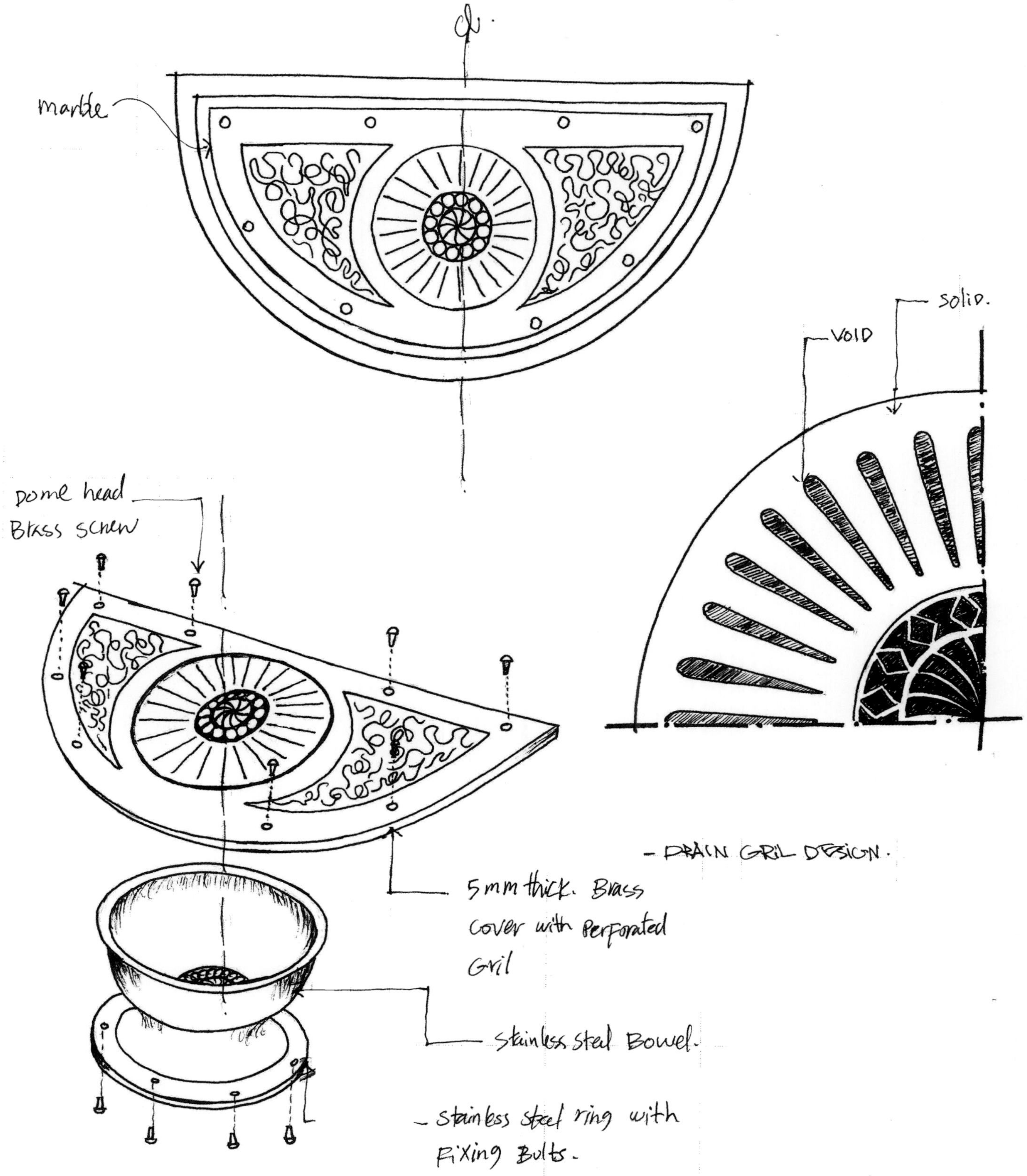

3.19
Succession of arches and columns in the inner space of *riwaq*

3.20
A northern corridor of the *riwaq* leading to the reading area

3.21
Series of columns and lancet arches allowing the entry of sunlight to the inner space of the *riwaq*

3.22
Domed ceiling of the *riwaq* from which a single-layer chandelier is suspended; also showing the *riwaq*'s exposure to the sunlight

3.23
A bottom-up view of the inner mottled arcade of the *mihrab*

3.24
A view of the upper point of the *mihrab*

consultation and reflection. This colonnade has a direct access to the ablution area, where the ablution is performed before entering the prayer hall. The *riwaq* draws upon the prayers and visitors to come together for dialogue, discussions and discourse. The *riwaq* of Imam Muhammad ibn Abdul Wahhab *masjid* is designed as a transitional space between the courtyard and other main spaces of the *masjid* like the prayer hall, the library, the reading and the ablution area. It is decorated with repetitive motives of traditional ornamentations framing the opening of lancet arch shape and brass chandeliers suspended from the centers of around 65 domes casing its roof.

Mihrab

Mihrab is an ornamental indentation in the wall of a mosque, which marks the direction of the *qibla* and varies in size and color. The *mihrab* of the Imam's *masjid* is shaped like a doorway with a GRC lancet arch, decorated by engraved circular pattern, glass mosaic tiles and calligraphy to make it prominently stand out. The height of the *mihrab* from inside reaches to almost 11 meters and it is cladded using white marble finishing. In the center of the upper part of the *mihrab* the word "Allah" is carved using the *Thuluth* script. It has been decorated from outside using two small half-circular domes above the flat roof. In addition to marking the *qibla*, the niche helps amplify the voice of the Imam during the congregational prayer.

Minbar

Minbar is a raised platform in the front area of a mosque, from which sermons or speeches are given. In addition to making the speaker visible to worshipers, the *minbar* helps amplify the voice of the speaker. In modern times, microphones are used for this purpose. The traditional *minbar* is a common element of Islamic mosque architecture throughout the world. It is a component where the art of wood engraving using Islamic geometrical patterns flourished.

In Imam Muhammad ibn Abdul Wahhab *masjid* two *minbar* are located to the right and left side of the *mihrab*, which marks the direction of the *qibla* for prayer. The two *minbar* are accessible from the

3.25
Ornamental indentation of *mihrab* and *minbar*

3.26
A drawing showing the carving and mottled details of *mihrab* and *minbar*

3:22
ASR
3:22

backside of the *mihrab* through a corridor that is linked via small gate to the outside podium of the *masjid*. White marble is used in cladding the *minbar* that is decorated with GRC and brass engraved screen of overlapping circular pattern. A solid purma teak decorates the wooden door leading to the steps of the *minbar* with brass belt and a carved pattern is adorning the bottom part of the *minbar*. The speaker walks up number of steps and either sits or stands on the *minbar* while addressing the worshipers.

Minaret

The minaret is a slim tower rising from a mosque, from which the *adhan* is called. Early mosques did not have minarets; the *adhan* was simply called from any high point near the mosque or from its roof. In modern times, microphones and speakers are often used to project the *adhan*, but minarets remain a common element in Islamic mosque architecture throughout the world. The minaret has become a symbol of the mosque and a visual tool by which the location of it can be determined within the fabric of a city. Minarets are always attached to the mosque, and vary in height, style and form. They may be designed to rise from a square, round, or octagonal base and are usually covered with a pointed roof. The minaret of the *masjid* of Imam Muhammad ibn Abdul Wahhab is the replica of the design concept of the minaret of old AlQubeib mosque with slender cylindrical form based on a stone footing including some small opening in the upper section for lighting and ventilation purpose. The cylindrical hull is covered and roofed using lobed form of dome with a wooden crescent on top of it directed toward *qibla*. The minaret is accessible through the courtyard using a stone staircase. The same concept of minaret using a different type of construction materials and finishing has been reproduced in the new mosque of 99 domes.

Library and Reading Area

The *masjid* of Imam Muhammad ibn Abdul Wahhab houses a library and reading area in addition to the *Qur'an* memorizing center for both men and women aiming to become not only a mosque used throughout the week for prayer but also a center for Islamic Studies and awareness. The female Qur'an memorizing hall is located in the mezzanine floor. It is accessible through the southern corridor and

3.27
A view of the *masjid*'s main gate and the minaret

3.28
Night view of the minaret on the north-eastern side of the *masjid*

3.29
A night time view from the courtyard (*sahn*) to the minaret

3.30
Design details of the *masjid*'s minaret

3.31
Hand-sketch showing the installation of light protection cover into the lobed dome of the minaret

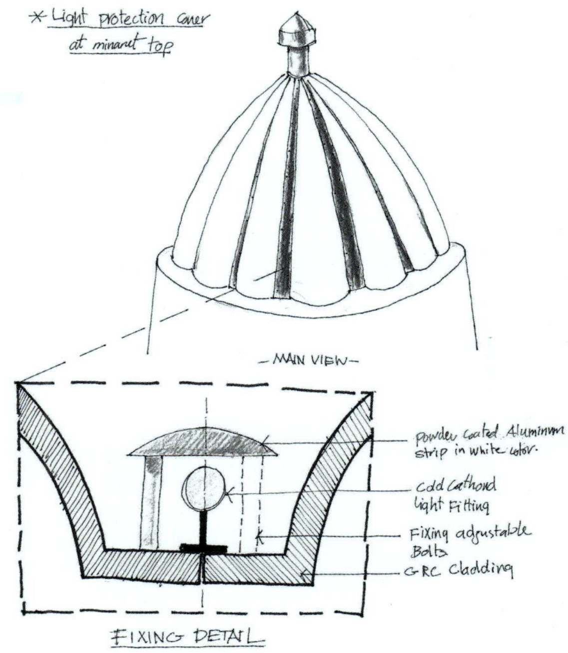

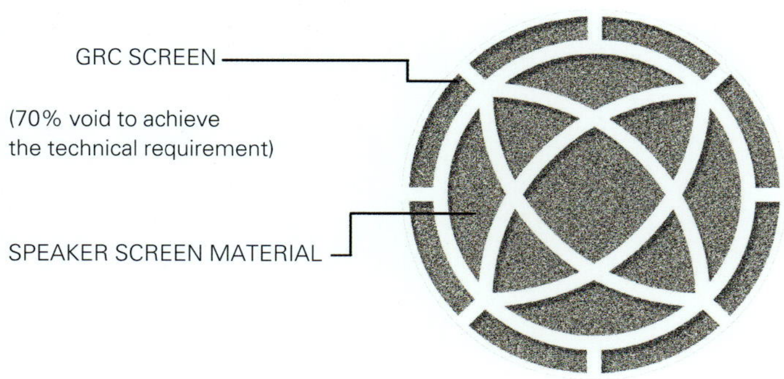

Pattern Design

Main View

Proposed GRC screen 6.nos in order to hide the speakers behind

3.32
The interior of the reading area located in the conic corner of the prayer hall

3.33
The marble cladded column
in the reading area

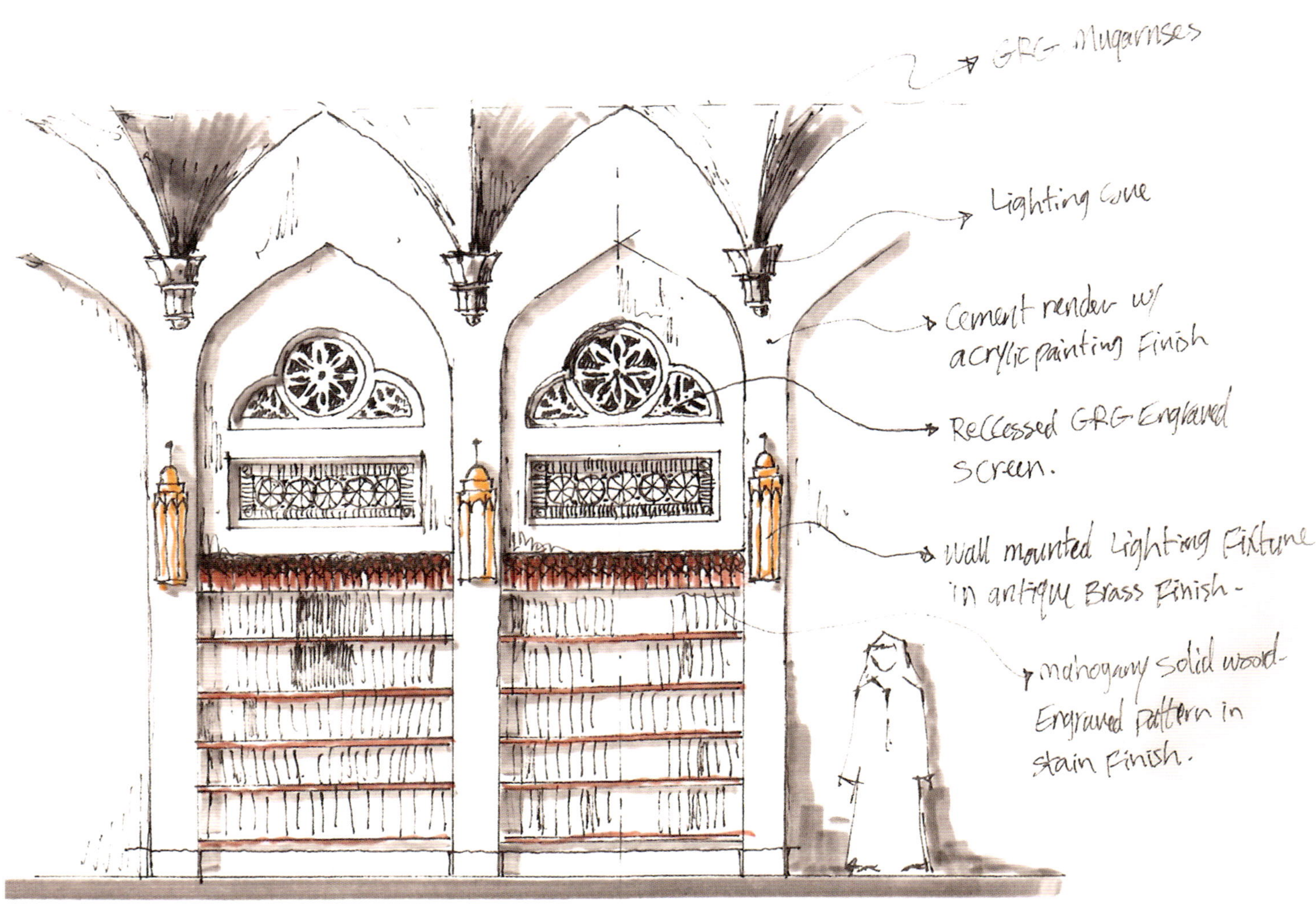

ELEVATION (1)

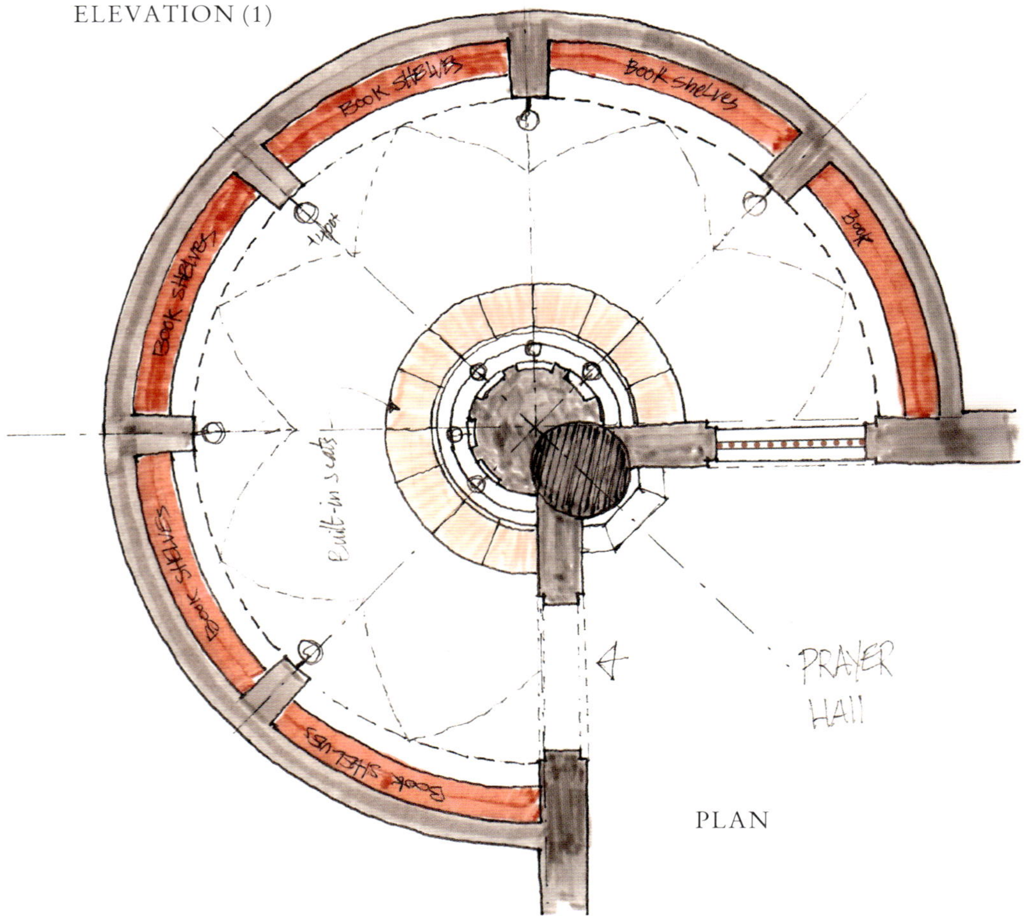

PLAN

3.34
Sketch showing the conceptual design of the reading area within the northern and southern conic corners of the prayer hall

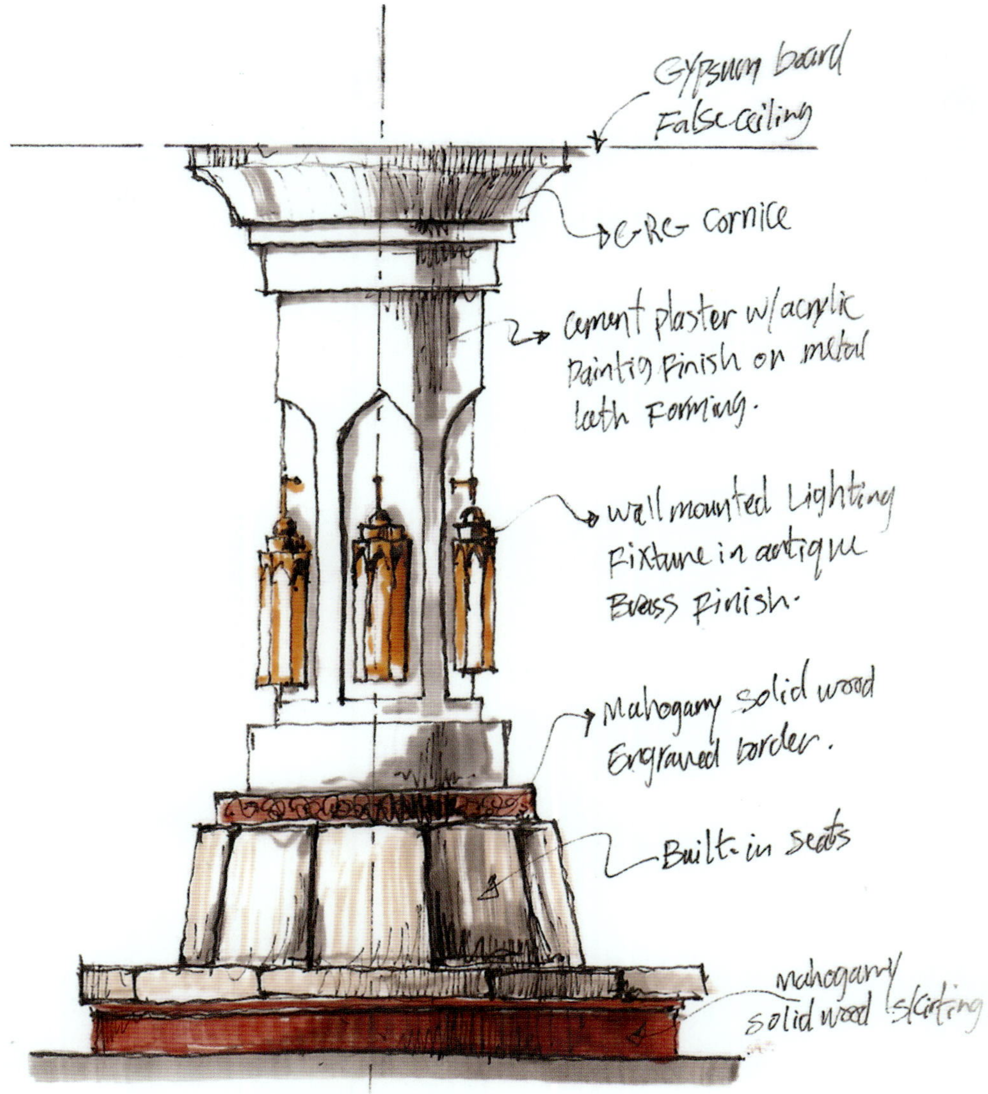

ELEVATION (2)

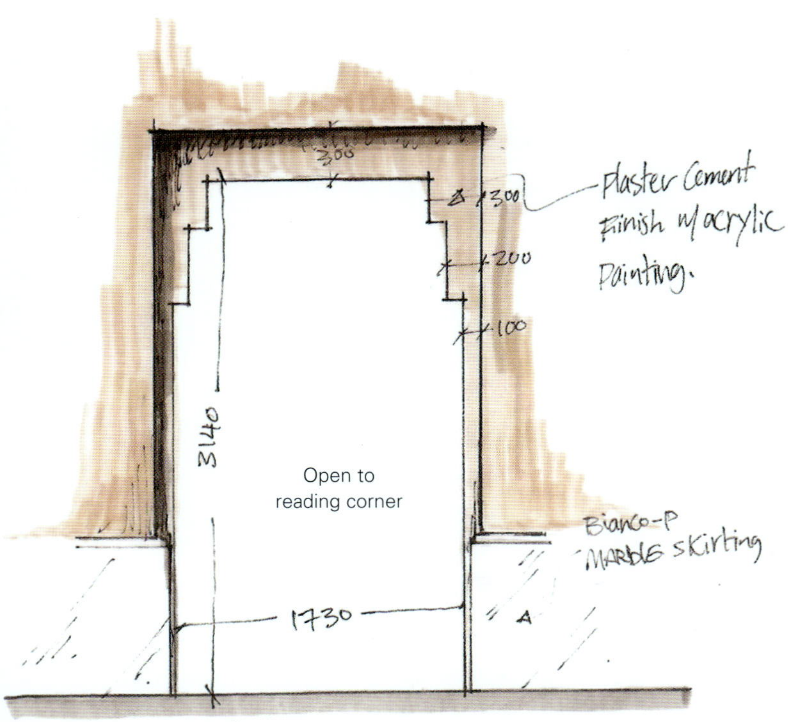

FRONT VIEW

Diffused light lighting fitting with a die-cast body that can be recessed directly into concrete

3.35
Zoomed-in shot of the decorative wooden panel of bookshelves fixed to the wall in the reading area

3.36–3.37
The interior of the library

3.38
The two-colored floor marble in combination with multi-colored mosaic decorating the female ablution area

3.39
The marble and mosaic decoration of the female wash area located in the ground level

has a capacity of 40 students. However, the male memorizing hall is located in the northern part of the *masjid* close to the Imam and speakers offices, serving 90 male students.

Mutawada'a

Mutawada'a is the place to perform *wudu* (ablution), the act of washing oneself, a ritual purification in Islam. The worshipers reach the *mutawada'a* through the northern corridors of the *masjid*, where the ablution space for 11 worshipers with special needs can be found also, reaching to the northern gate of the *masjid* that leads to the *riwaq*. The female entry gate is directed toward a closed hallway separated from the *riwaq* creating the level of privacy needed and directly connected from two sides to the ablution area dedicated to the women, with capacity of 80 worshipers, through lift and stairs that lead to the female prayer hall in the mezzanine floor. However, the male ablution area that is located within the basement and accessible via lifts and staircases in both sides of the northern corridor connects to the utility buildings through an underground tunnel. The male *mutawada'a* serves 317 worshipers.

Sabeel

Sabeel is an Arabic word used in Islam to name a "spring" or a "channel" of living water. It also means "the way". However, in this book, it refers to a place that provides potable water to the thirsty passers-by. Believing that the water is one of the great graces of Allah, Muslims in Islamic cities devote and offer water to passers-by perusing and rejoicing for Allah's favor and (His) grace as per the following verses of holy Qur'an.

> "Verily! As for those who believe and do righteous deeds, certainly! We shall not suffer to be lost the reward of anyone who does his (righteous) deeds in the most perfect manner."
> (al-Kahf 18: 31).

The four *sabeel* of Imam Muhammad ibn Abdul Wahhab *masjid* are designed in distinctive manner using Islamic architectural features, and are located in an outer yard (podium) in front of the great gate of the

Section C–C

3.40
The design of the interior space of the male rest rooms area

3.41
Sketch showing the detail of interior spaces of the male rest room and ablution area located in the basement

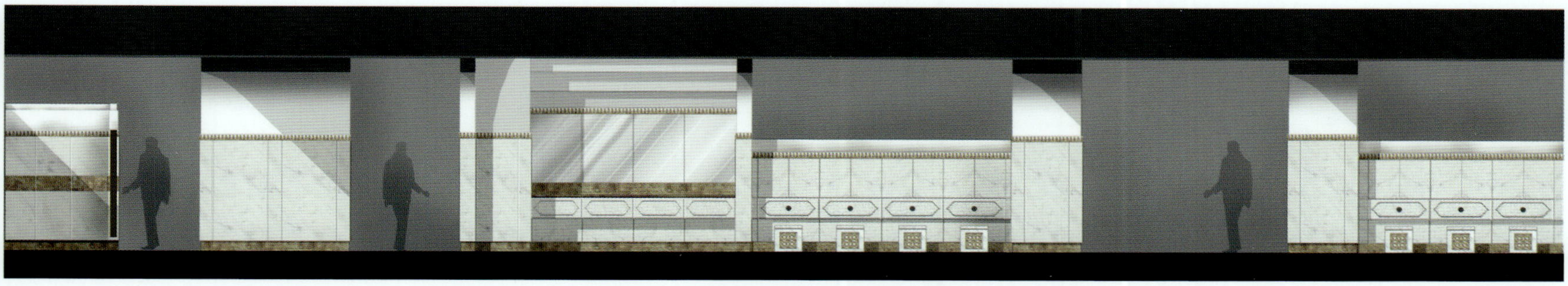

Section A–A

Section B–B

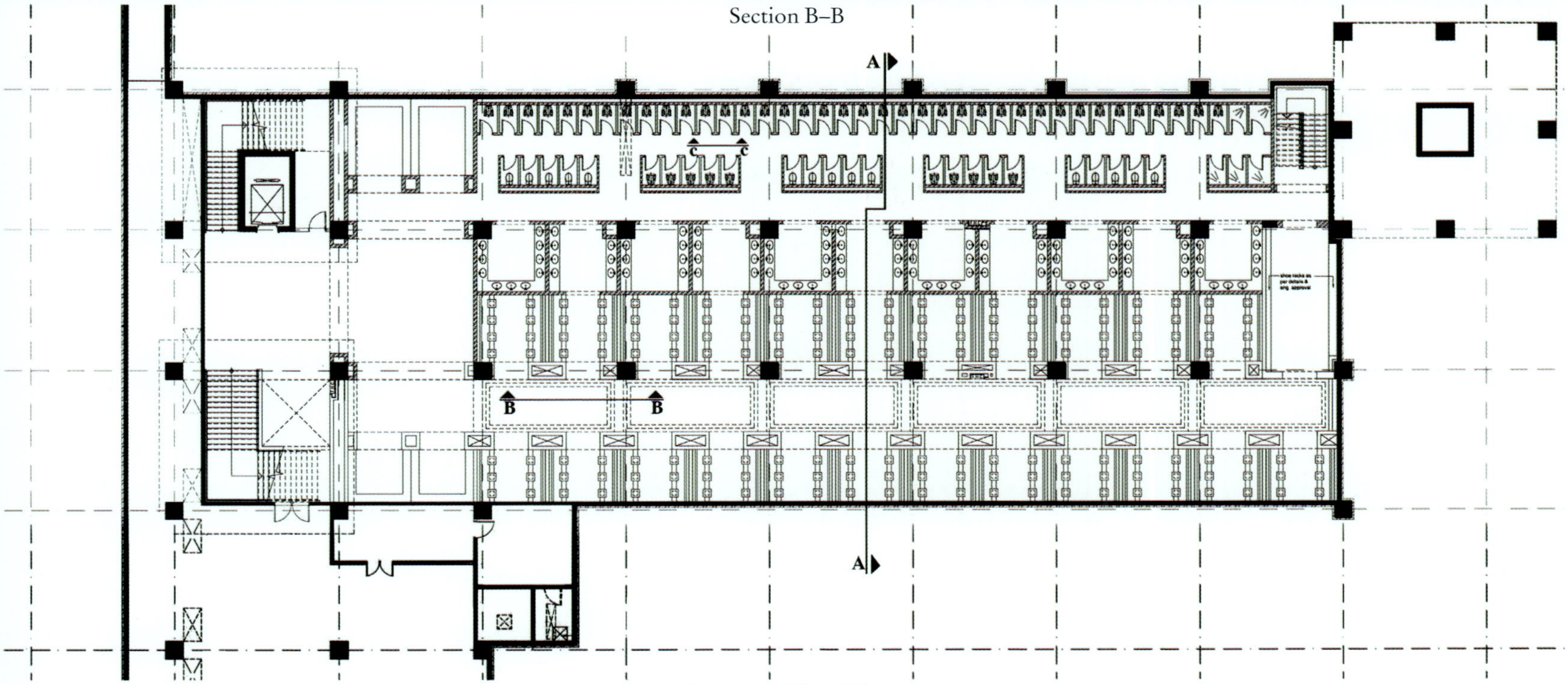

Basement Floor Plan

3.42
Overview of the inner ablution area

3.43
The water tap fixed to the mottled marble wall of the ablution area

3.44
An inner hallway leading to the wash and ablution area

masjid. Each *sabeel* is built using fine finishing of sandstone and roofed with a small dome. The front and back facades are designed using red marble cladding with engraved traditional patterns and inner screen of glass mosaic inlay with an Arabic words *Bismillah al-Rahman al-Rahim;* meaning "in the name of God, the Most Gracious, the Most Merciful"; in the upper part of the cladding using *Thuluth* script.

Masjid's Building Structure

The *masjid* is highly distinguished by its unique building structure and uses of arcades (a succession of arches, each counter-thrusting the next, supported by columns or piers) and 99 domes used in roofing the aisle of *qibla*, arcades, *mihrab* and *sabeel*.

Arcades (Columns and Arches)
An arcade is a succession of arches, each counter-thrusting the next, supported by columns, piers, or a covered walkway enclosed by a line of such arches on one or both sides. In warmer or wet climates, exterior arcades provide shelter for pedestrians. The arcade of the Imam Muhammad ibn Abdul Wahhab *masjid* is designed using the lancet or Gothic type of arches which are cladded by gypsum and create a domed ceiling space adorned by the multi-layered brass chandeliers.

The Significance of 99 Domes
The number of domes, 99, has a significant religious meaning as it illustrates the special 99 names of Allah. The two *sahih* collected this *hadith* of Prophet Muhammad (*pbuh*) saying:

> "Verily, Allah has ninety-nine names, a hundred less one; whoever counts (and preserves) them, will enter Paradise."
> (*Sahih* Muslim: 2677)

This *hadith* actually conveys that anyone who really believes in these ninety-nine attributes of Allah and always remembers them truly will be compelled to live a good life avoiding all the unseemly acts that may emanate from him in case he forgets the Lord. Thus, he, by remembering His Lord with all His attributes, will become entitled to enter Paradise because of the God-fearing life he leads in this world.

3.45
The traditional design of the *sabeel*

3.46
The *sabeel* in front of the main entrance of the *masjid*

3.47
Hand-sketch of the *sabeel*

3.48
The plan and decorative elevation of the *sabeel*

3.49
A close-up of the *sabeel* showing the details of the carved marble and tiled mosaic

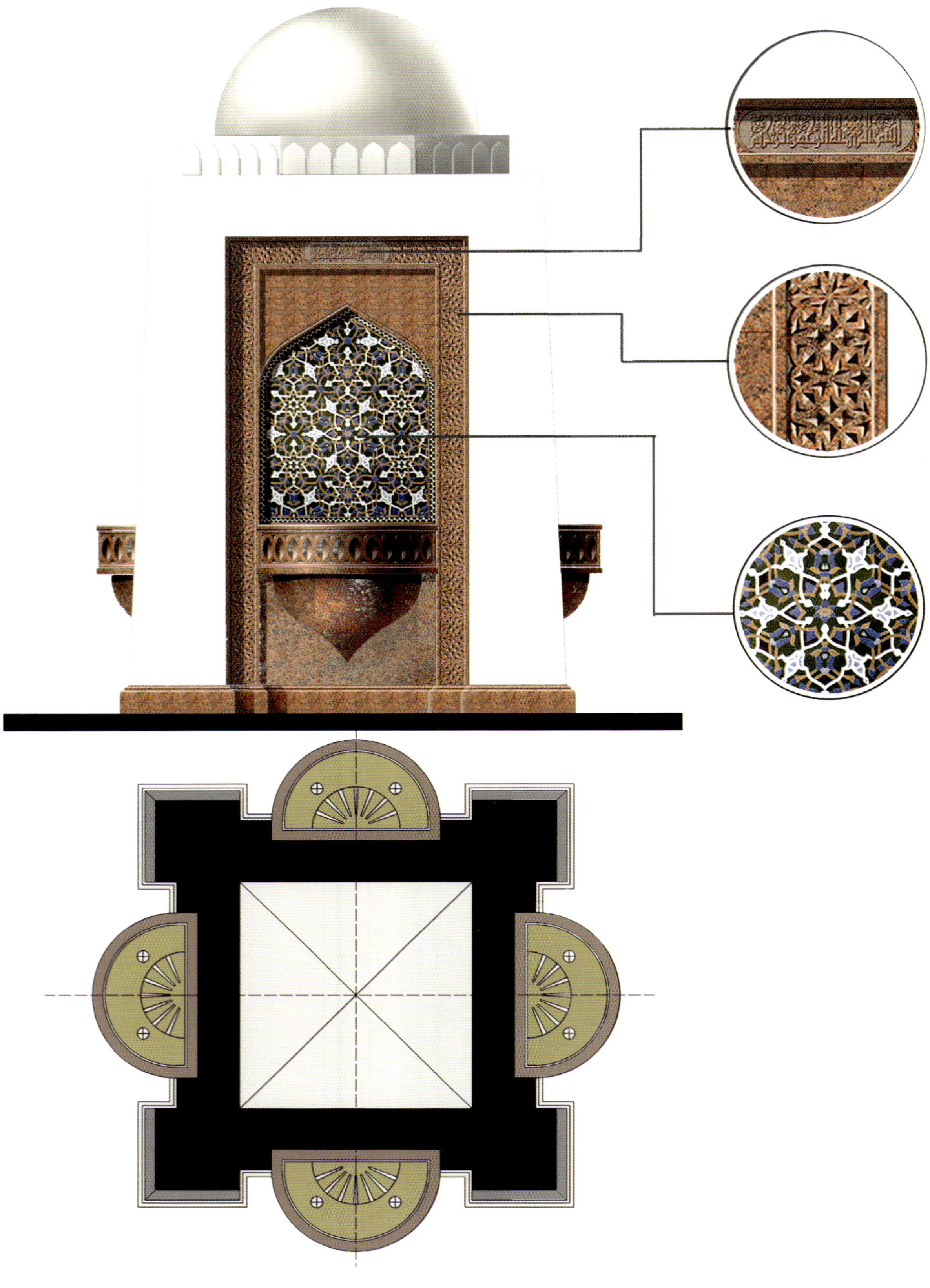

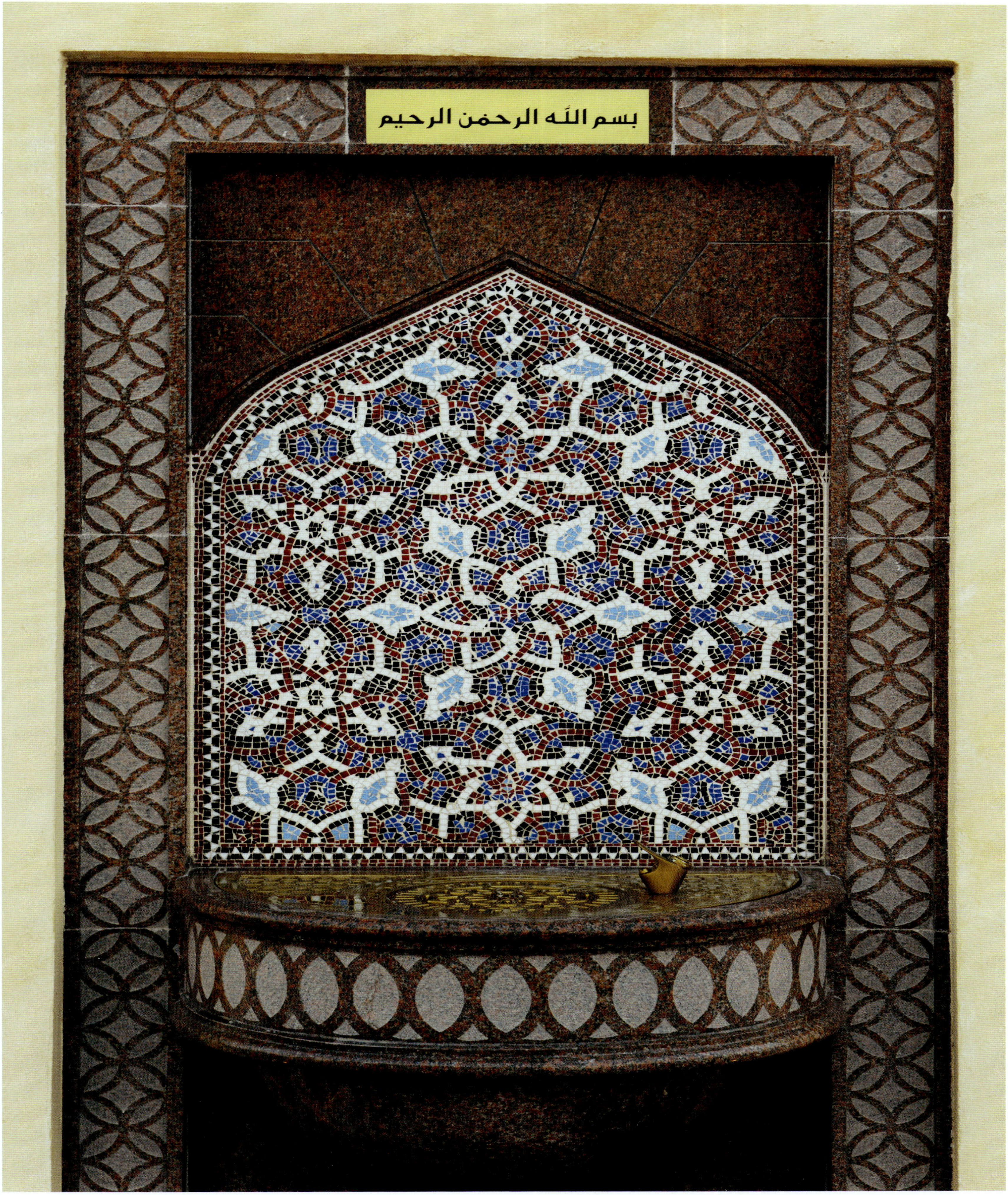
بسم الله الرحمن الرحيم

Many mosques are decorated with a domed rooftop, particularly in the Middle East. This architectural element holds no spiritual or symbolic significance, and is purely of aesthetic and structural nature. The interior of a dome is usually highly decorated with floral, geometric and other type of patterns and ornaments using variety of interior finishing. The *masjid* of Imam Muhammad ibn Abdul Wahhab is adorned by 99 domes, which are used for both structural and aesthetical purposes and are dispersed on top of the mosque's basic elements:

- 28 domes roof the prayer area raised up to almost 29.15 meters above the prayer hall ground level;
- 65 domes of smaller size cover the arcades surrounding the courtyard;
- 4 domes are on top of the four *sabeel*;
- 2 domes are on top of *mihrab*.

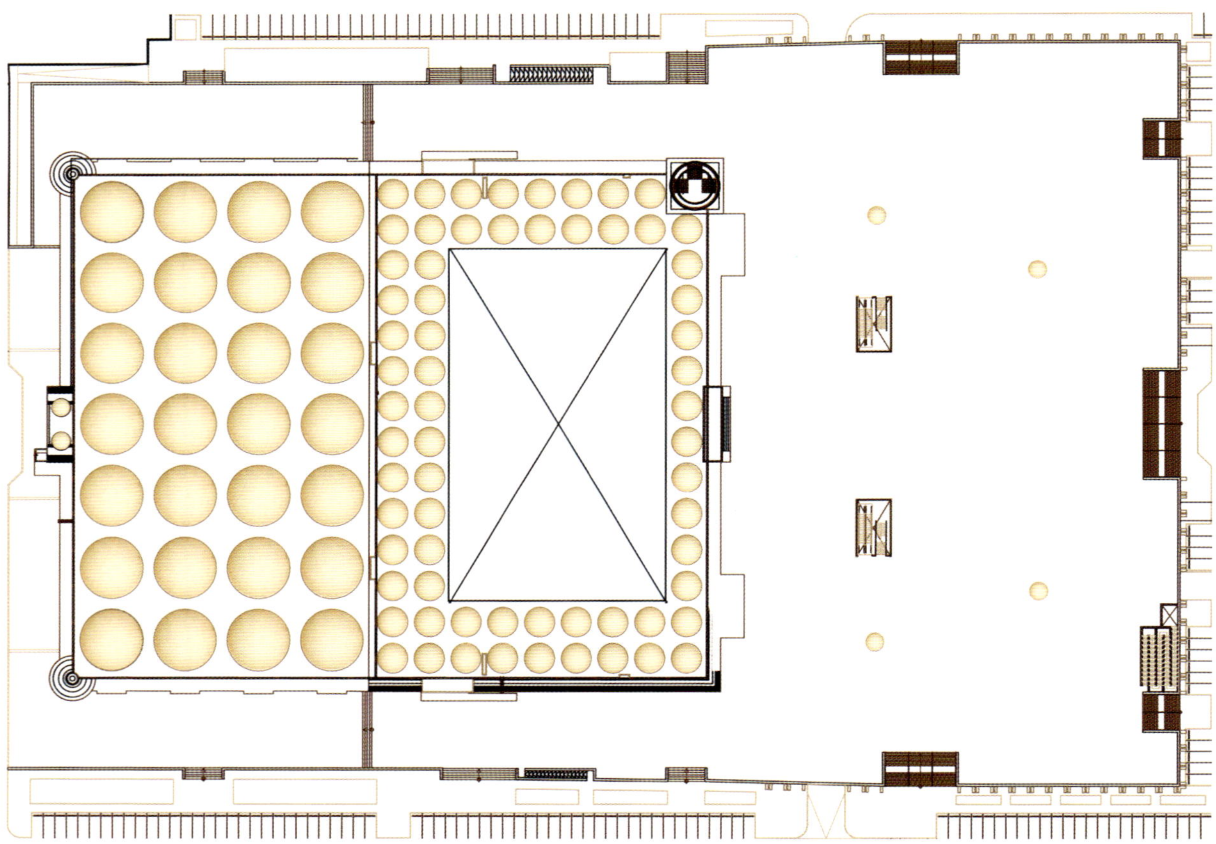

28 domes roof the prayer area

2 domes roof the *mihrab*

65 domes roof the *riwaq*

4 domes case the top of *sabeels*

3.50
Key plan indicating number of domes in the prayer hall, *riwaq*, *mihrab* and *sabeel* of the *masjid*

3.51
An antique rug/frame illustrating the 99 beautiful names of Allah from which the number of domes roofing the *masjid* are inspired

Chapter IV

Artistic and Aesthetic Values of the Masjid

The Link between Art and Architecture in Islam

The integration of art and artifacts in Islamic architecture was so evident in different eras of the Islamic civilization. It is also well manifested in different building types from humble *sabeel* to a sophisticated *madrassa* or mosque. As Hillenbrand (1998) and Grabar (1988) brilliantly argue, art and architecture in Islam are organically integrated so that the distinction between the two becomes impossible. Mosques are considered to socially inspire projects where an important connection is established between people and place. Physical and psychological needs are considered, and art and aesthetics features are used to fulfill such needs. Mosques give the highest comfort that satisfy the psychological tranquility of the users in different cultural environments. Precisely in the case of the mosque, artistic interventions are used to convey a message of tranquility and serenity alluding to the atmosphere of the paradise, the destination for every truthful Muslim. In Qur'an, around 120 passages mention and describe the Paradise (Al Janna) as a beautiful serene place, as mentioned in the following verse:

> "For them will be Gardens of Eternity; beneath them rivers will flow; they will be adorned therein with bracelets of gold and they will wear green garments of fine silk and heavy brocade; they will recline therein on raised thrones. How good the recompense! How beautiful a couch to recline on?". (al-Kahf 18:31)

This is where the most of the mosques, just as is the case with the *masjid* of Imam Muhammad ibn Abdul Wahhab, envisioned their aesthetics features of motifs and ornamentation, symbolically portraying the Paradise garden. Architects, in the past and even today, have made use of local artisans and local artists to adorn interiors and exteriors of the mosques. As symbol of Islamic architecture, a mosque plays an important role in reflecting the superiority of Allah the Almighty. There are many ways in reflecting this notion and one of them is through the high quality of aesthetic value. Aesthetic value in Islamic art and architecture is usually portrayed through the highly decorative and intricate geometric and floral patterns and calligraphy, unlike the architects of contemporary mosques who are usually focused on the majestic look of the exterior of the mosques and leave the manipulation of the interior space to the

4.1
Night-time view of the main eastern brass metal gateway of the *masjid*

4.2
Detailed sketch of the main gateway decorated by numerous local patterns

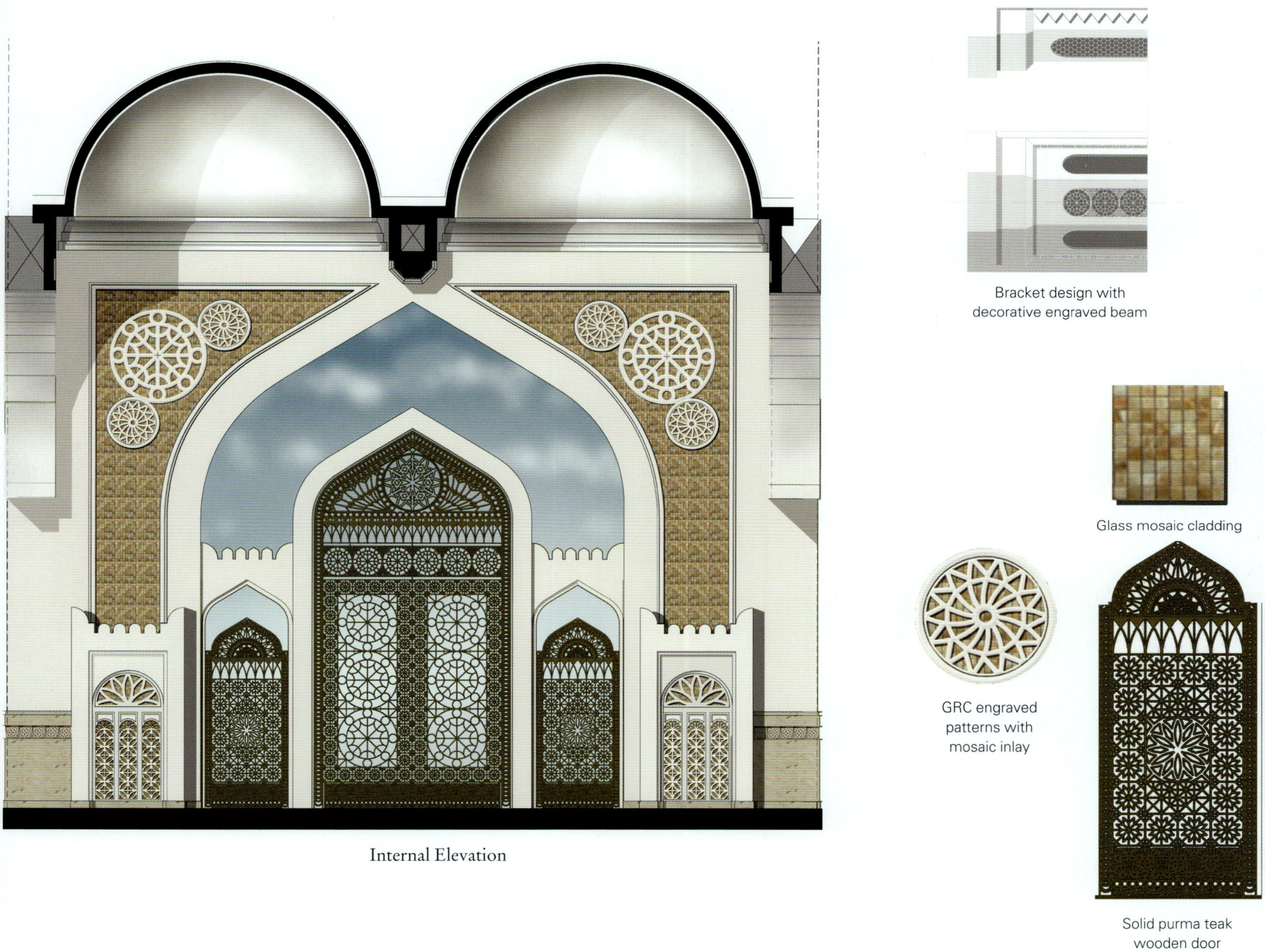

4.3
The main entrance for women on southern side of the *masjid* decorated using combination of circular and square overlaying pattern

4.4
The close-up of the entrance door for women

4.5
The secondary entrance to the prayer hall for men made of carved purma teak wood and mottled glass

users. The lead architect of the Masjid of Imam Muhammad ibn Abdul Wahhab, precisely designed the artistic features focusing on the ornamentation of the mosque's interior; so that decoration of the place of worship is controlled and not overpowering, which might result in taking away from the intended humbleness and modesty.

Openings: Doors, Windows and Screens

Examining the history of Islamic architecture reveals that every single component of buildings and spaces was used as a physical opportunity to diffuse the concept of beauty. Highly distinguished among essential elements of any mosque are the different types of openings. Elements like doors, windows and screens allow for the innovative use of materials like wood, glass, and metal. More importantly, such elements are primarily decorated using geometrical or floral elements. The case of *masjid* of Imam Muhammad ibn Abdul Wahhab is very interesting as the climatic conditions forced the architect to resort to more solid façades with a limited number of openings. Yet every external window or door were seen as an opportunity to exhibit the distinguished artistic features and aesthetics values associated with Islamic and Gulf architecture. The *masjid* of Imam Muhammad ibn Abdul Wahhab comprises a number of hard teak wooden carved doors that are ornately hand-crafted and studded with antique brass. Stressing the handicrafts and the role of artisans is adding to the value of the design as mosques were seen as an arena for local artists and craftsmen to show their talent and creativity. There are also iron doors, wooden and GRC screens, mottled glass and wooden windows, and other openings which are adorned with screens designed by using a selective number of geometric patterns. Unique rhythm is achieved by the use of discreet motifs created by repetition of basic geometric elements.

Geometrical Patterns and Calligraphy

Geometric patterns and calligraphy are most commonly used as decoration in the Islamic art (Grabar, 1988; Sutton, 2007). Whether used in isolation or in combination with different type of ornamentation, geometric patterns are popularly associated with Islamic art. Geometrical ornamentations are supporting

4.6
Small purma teak wooden door decorated using floral pattern carving and brass bolts

4.7
The highly ornate main entrance to the *musalla* decorated using the floral patter carving as well as brass door hinges and handles

4.8
The hand-sketch of floral patterns used in decorating door leaf

4.9
The close-up of finished floral wooden carving used in decorating door leaf

4.10
The brass handles

4.11
The hand-sketch showing the plan, section and isometric view of the lever handle

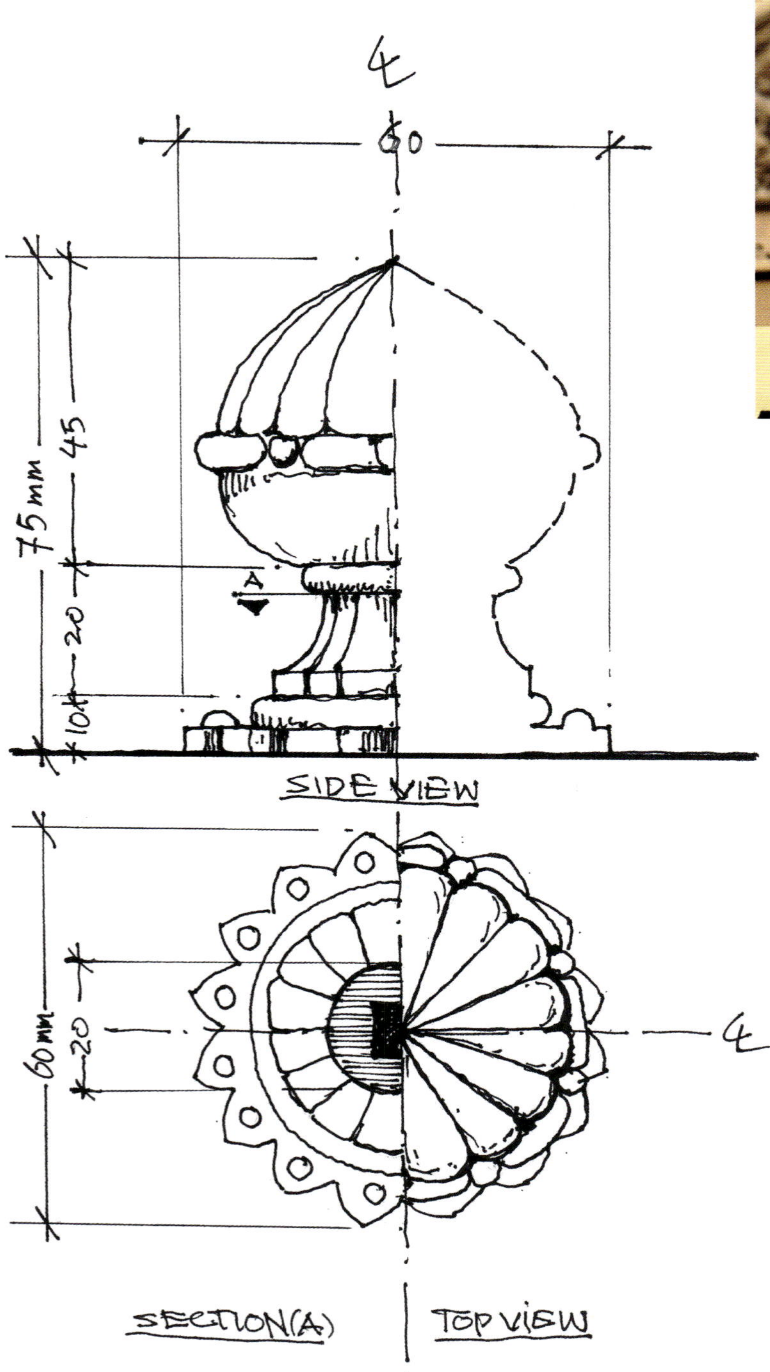

4.12
Finished antique brass knob decorated with a combination of local circular pattern

4.13
A sketch illustrating the perspective and profile of cast antique brass knob

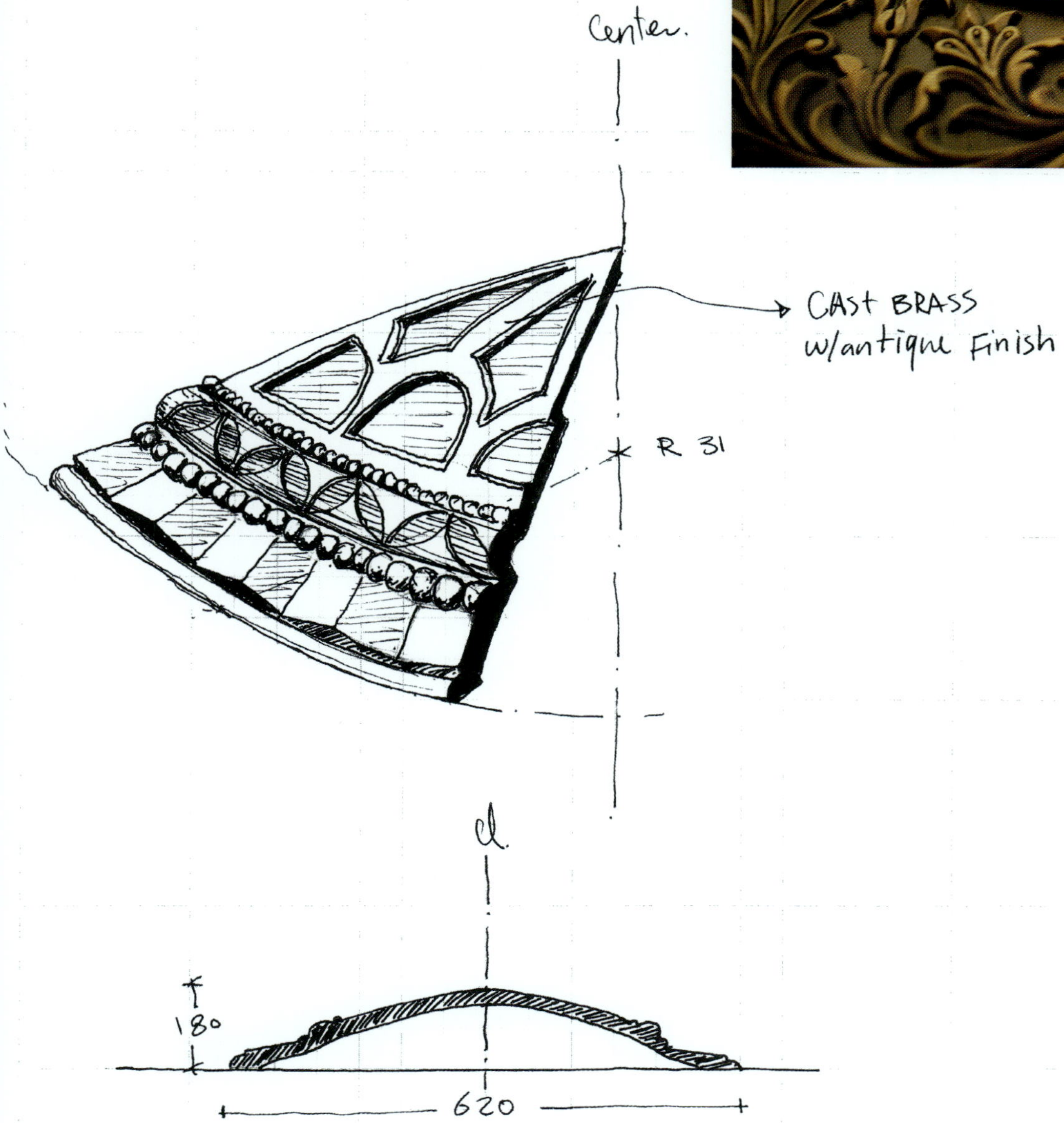

4.10
The close-up of the door leading to the prayer hall for men

4.15
The sketch showing the details of the floral ornamentation used to decorate the leaf of the prayer hall's main entrance for men

4.16
The detail of the solid cast brass pull handles

4.17
The hand-sketch of solid cast brass pull handles

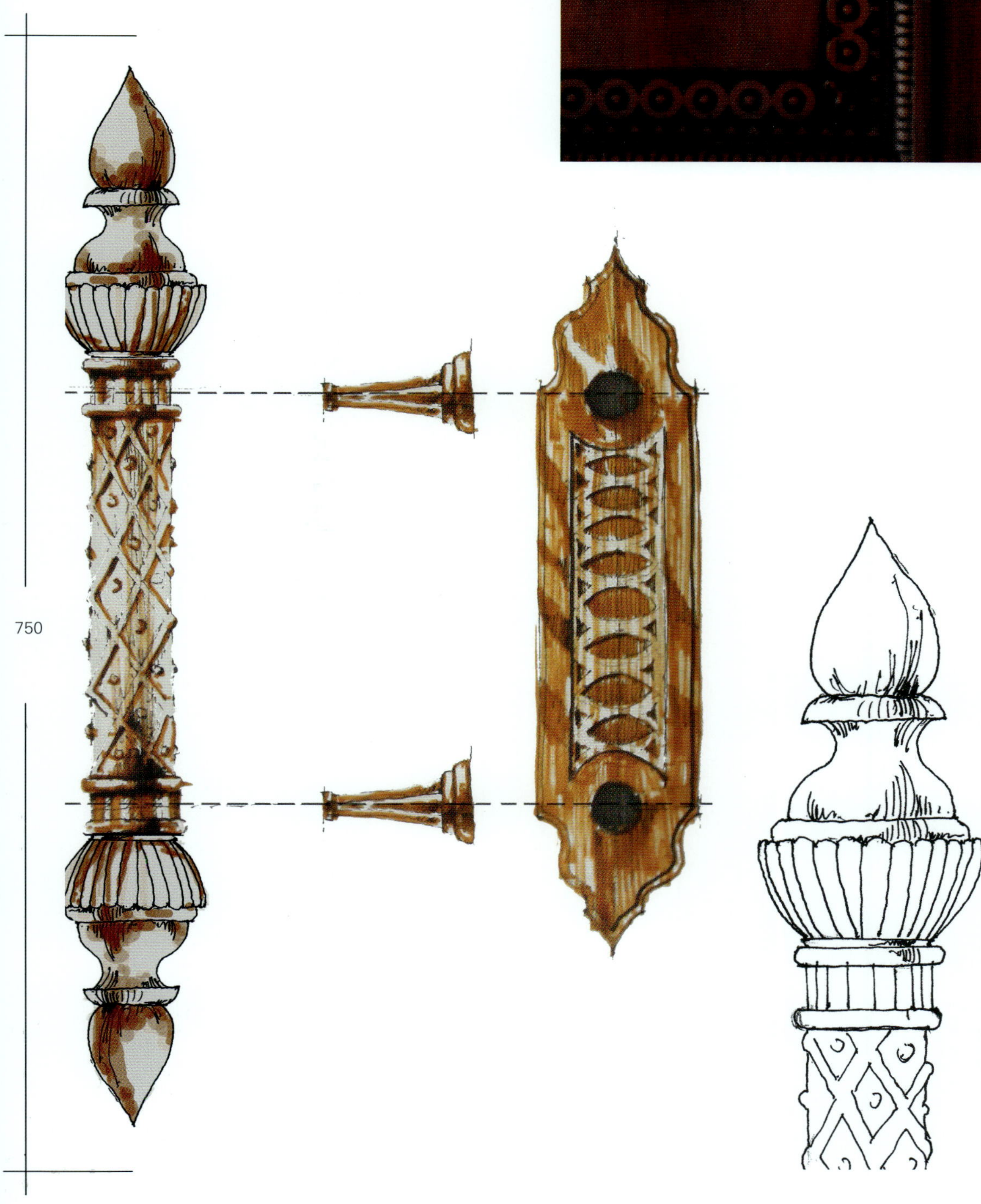

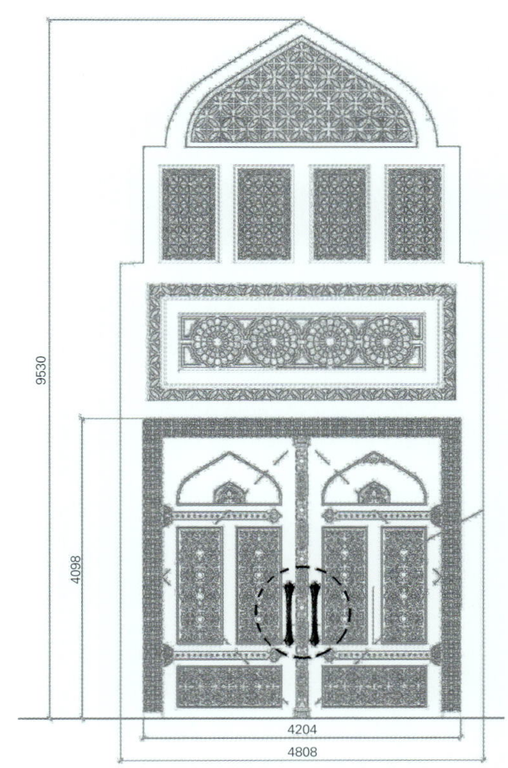

4.18
The secondary entrance door to the prayer hall

4.19
The sketch showing the details of the ornamentation used in conspicuous porch of secondary entrances of the prayer hall

4.20
The sketch showing the details of the solid cast brass door's pivot

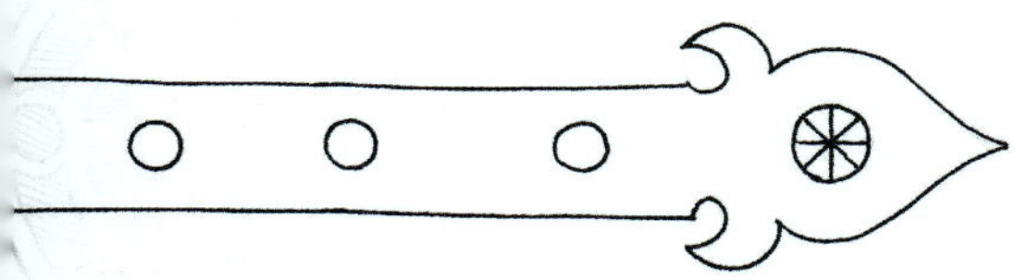

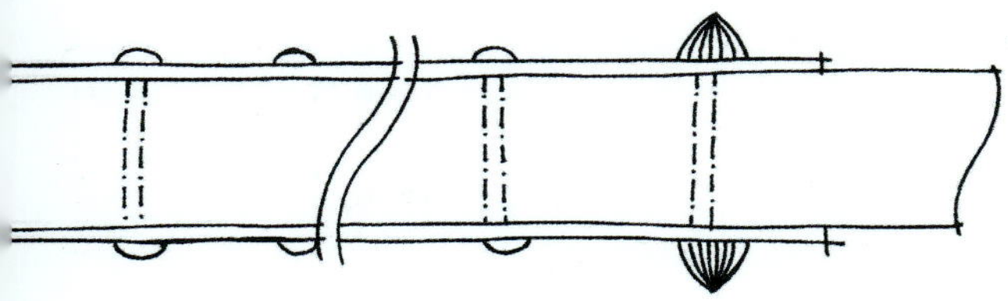

خطر الكهرباء
ELECTRICAL
HAZARD

4.21
The wooden carving and calligraphy etching of the door below the *minbar*

4.22
The view from the inside of the prayer hall

4.23
The close-up of the entrance from the inside of the prayer hall

4.24
A sketch illustrating the use of the basic colors in a mottled glass in the door leaf and upper board framing the doors

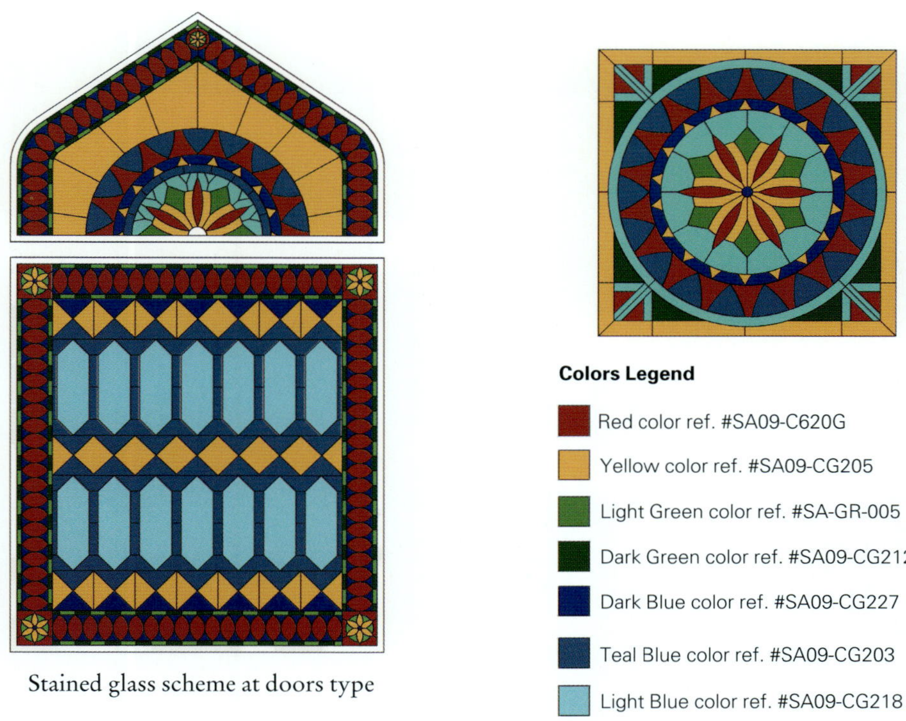

Stained glass scheme at doors type

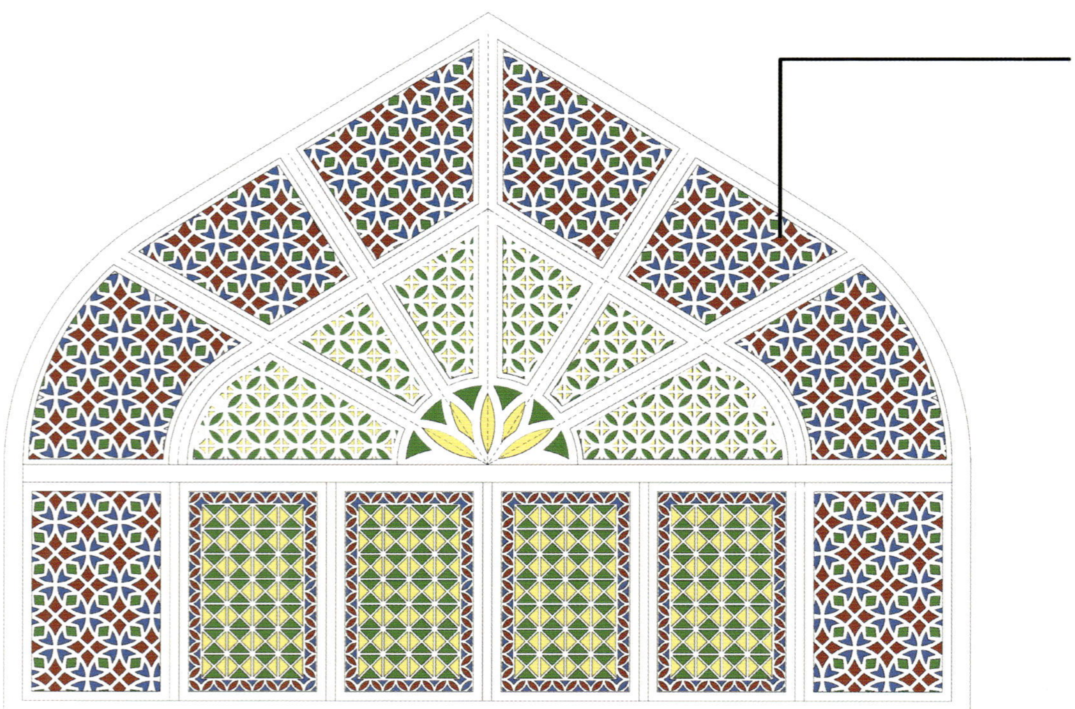

Additional GRC screen layer with colored glass inlay

Colors Legend

- Red color ref. #SA09-C620G
- Yellow color ref. #SA09-CG205
- Light Green color ref. #SA-GR-005
- Dark Green color ref. #SA09-CG212
- Dark Blue color ref. #SA09-CG227
- Teal Blue color ref. #SA09-CG203
- Light Blue color ref. #SA09-CG218

4.25
An image of the inner side of the prayer hall secondary entrance with prominent mottled GRC panel

4.26
The sketch illustrating the patterns and colors used in decorating the upper panel board of the inner side of the prayer hall secondary entrance

4.27
The sketch illustrating the patterns and colors been used in decorating the GRC screens placed along the hallways and inner corridors

4.28
The GRC carved screens and mottled marble flooring present in the corners of the hallways

4.29
The shadow of patterned brass metallic screen ornates the flooring of the inner space of the *riwaq* and hallways

4.30
The patterned brass metallic screen with lancet arch and upper GRC ornamentation ornate the *sahn* of the *masjid*

4.31
A combination of local pattern used in decorating the metallic brass screens enclosing the courtyard of the *masjid*

4.32
An inner section of the ornamentation used in transition point dominated by lancet arch and great use of GRC patterned panels

4.33
An inner section depicting the scheme of the ornamentation used in transition point dominated by lancet arch and great use of golden mosaic tiles

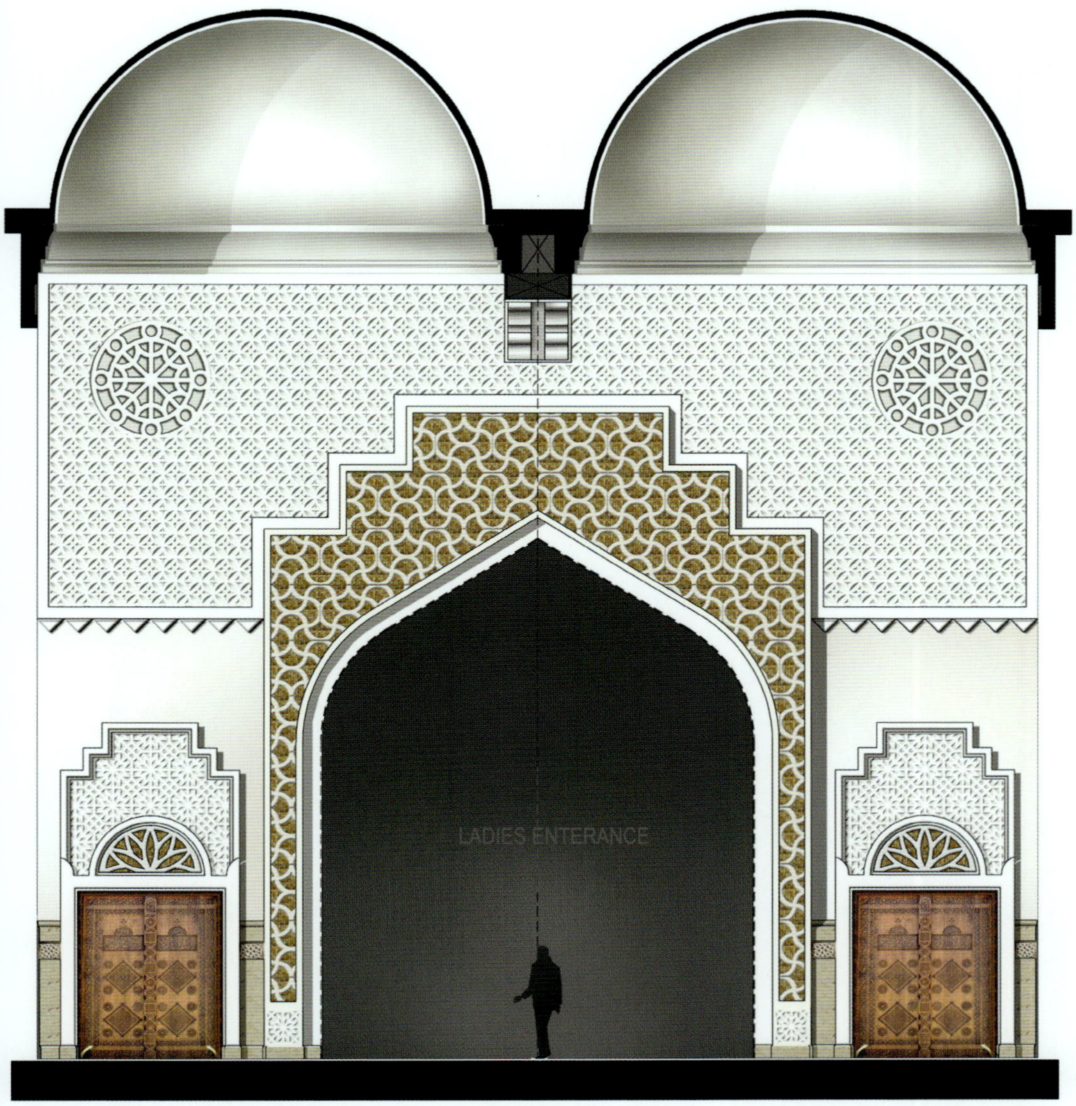

Internal Elevation

Bracket design with decorative engraved beam

GRC engraved pattern with mosaic inlay

GRC engraved patterns

Solid purma teak wooden door

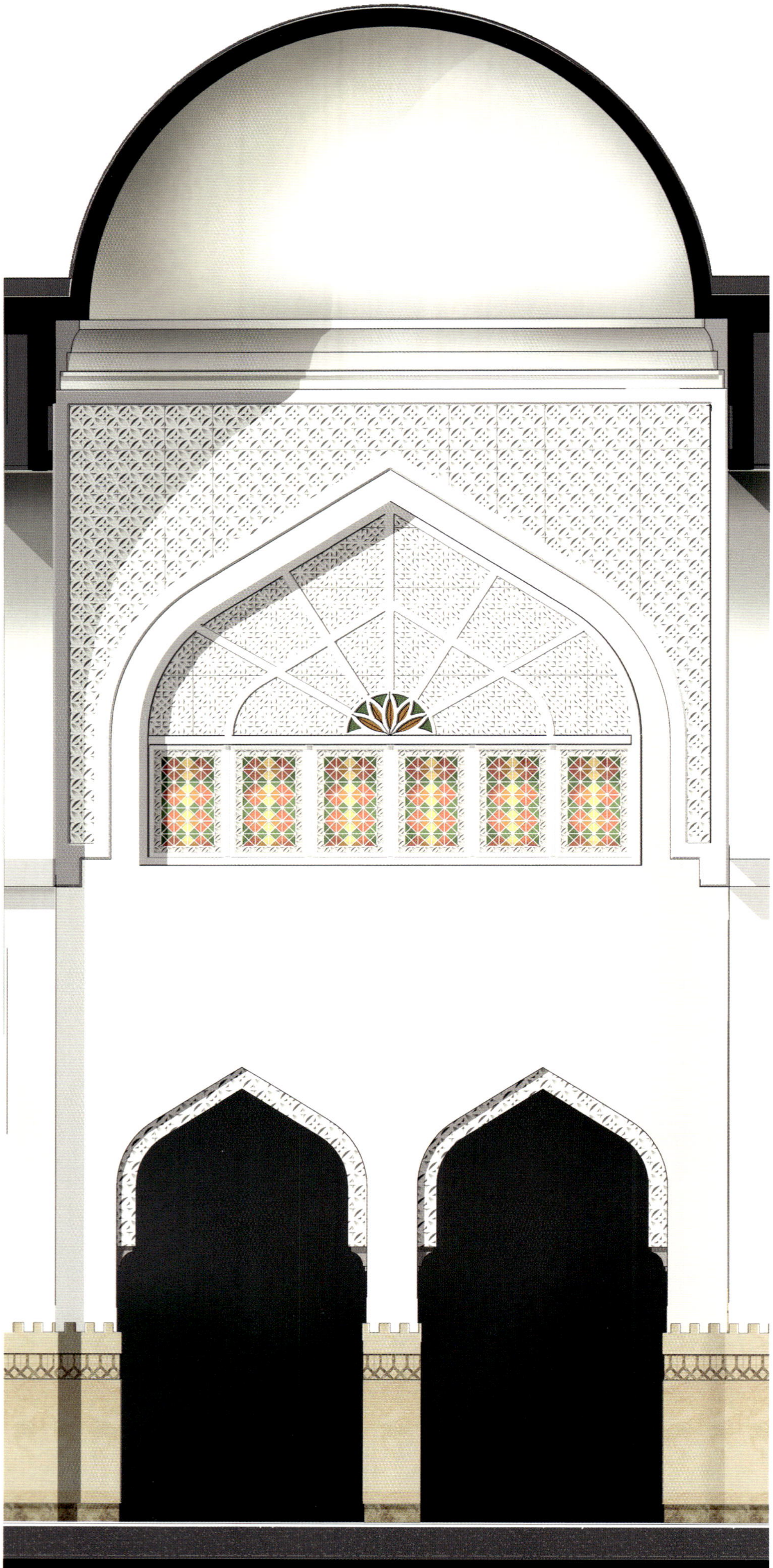

4.34
Rendered sketch of one of the GRC screens mottled using the inlay of golden mosaic

4.35
The combination of colors used in decorating the screens within the library and reading area of the *masjid*

4.36
The close view of the central upper side of the screens inside the library and reading area of the *masjid*

4.37
The mixture of colored glass fixed within the GRC screens decorating the inner side walls of the hallways leading to the library and reading area

4.38
The grooved pattern cast-off in decorating some inner walls of the *masjid*

4.39
The perforated wooden screen with mixture of local patterns that are used in screening the mezzanine floor *musalla*

4.40–4.43
Sketches of some of the local patterns derived by overlaying geometrical shapes like circle and square that are used in decorating the inner and outer spaces of the *masjid*

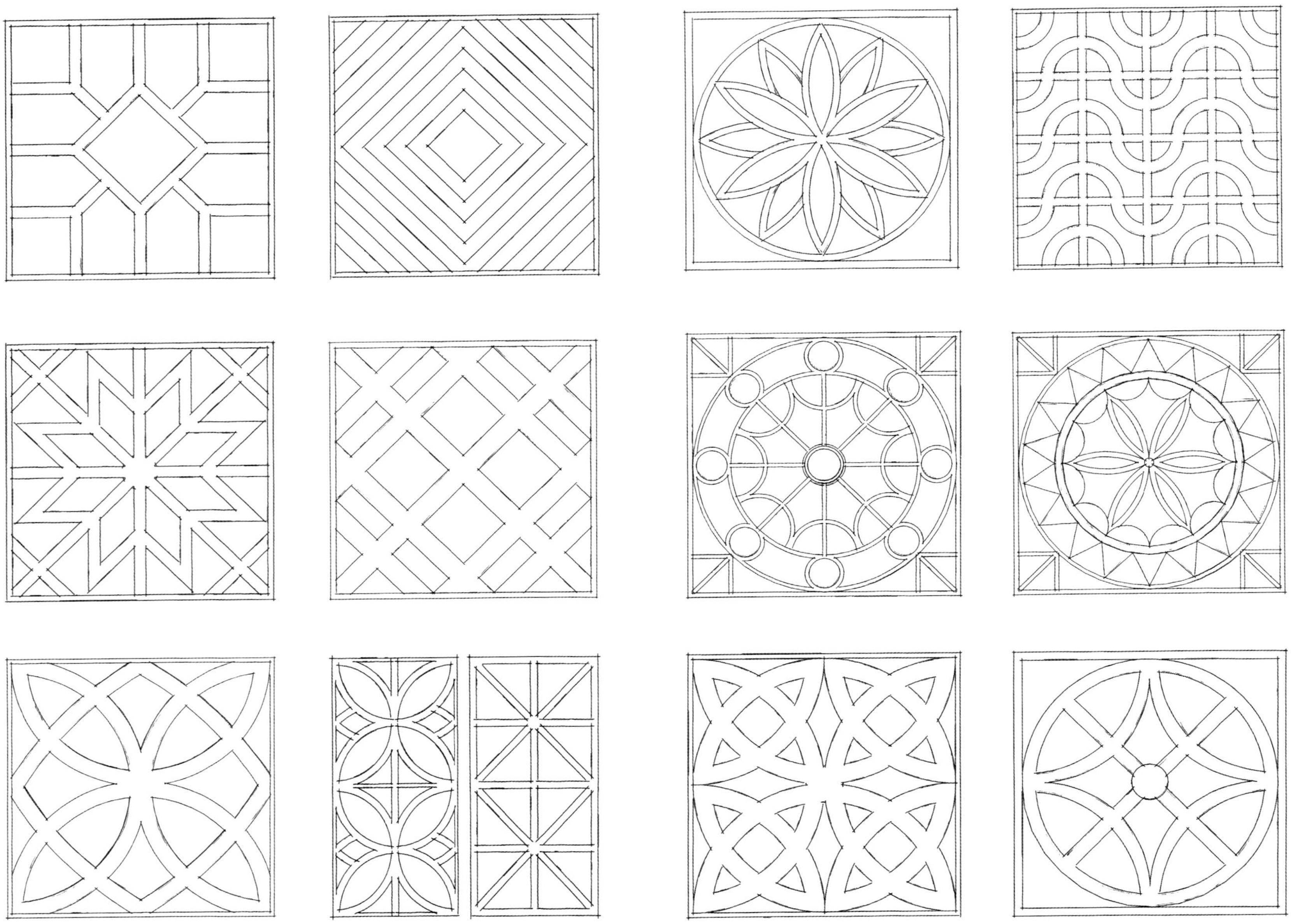

4.44
Sketch of some of the local patterns derived by overlaying geometrical shapes like circle and square that are used in decorating the inner and outer spaces of the *masjid*

4.45
Sketch showing the detailed illustration of patterns used in panel framing the secondary entrances of the *musalla*

4.46
The close-up of the finished antique-looking solid brass door handle

4.47
The decorated brass metallic door leaf of the *Qur'an* shelves embedded into the base of the pillars

and enhancing the spiritual atmosphere of any mosque. While it stimulates the mind to think of God, it is not distracting the worshipers or getting them away from their spiritual immersion. In the *masjid* of Imam Muhammad ibn Abdul Wahhab, the artistic elements are appropriated using the typical regional patterns found in old gypsum carvings and ornamentations all around the Arabian Gulf, mostly in Bahrain, Kuwait, United Arab Emirates, Qatar, and south of Iran. At the present time, these geometric patterns are manipulated and elaborated in Glass Fiber Reinforced Concrete (GRC), marble tiles, door carvings, and screen cutting. Inventing new visual elements that stress the importance of unity and order can be also traced in the contemporary works of local and regional artists present in buildings around the Gulf. As stated by Qatari artist Mohammed Ali Abdullah in his book *Gypsum Ornamentation in Gulf*, these patterns are generated commonly from simple forms like circle or square or the combination of both forms. The patterns are specifically named after being ornately developed by overlapping circles and squares in the ornamentations that resemble and relate to some culturally known symbols (Abdullah, 1985). In the *masjid* of Imam Muhammad ibn Abdul Wahhab, geometric shapes are combined, duplicated, interweaved, and arranged in intricate combinations, becoming one of the distinguishable features of the mosque. This process allows for a remarkable amount of freedom in the repetition and complexity, while offering the possibility of infinite growth. In terms of their abstractness, repetitiveness, and symmetry, the selected geometric patterns have much in common with the so-called arabesque style seen in many

4.48
The decorated brass metallic door leaf of the *Qur'an* shelves embedded into the base of the pillars with Arabic *Thuluth* script carved on its lever handles

botanical designs in masterpieces of architecture around the Islamic world. The four basic shapes, or "repeat units," from which the more complicated patterns are constructed are: circles and interlaced circles; squares or four-sided polygons; the universal star shape, ultimately derived from squares and triangles inscribed in a circle; and different polygons.

Calligraphic ornamentation also appears in combination with geometric patterns. This is considered to be the ultimate skill that transformed the words of the *Qur'an* into a visual work of art (Serageldin, 1996; Sutton, 2007). There are many calligraphy styles commonly used across the region such as *diwani, riq'a, ta'liq* and *nasta'liq*, but in the *masjid* of 99 domes only two scripts of *naskh* and *thuluth* are used and are mostly found in decorating walls, doors, and screens of the mosque. The art of calligraphy is expressed in the form of simply joined letters conveying messages of specific *Quranic* verses. The simplest form is *Naskh* script, which is then reordered so that letters can be angulated: as in the oldest *Kufic* script; or stretched, prolonged, bent, thickened, overlapped, and complicated: as in the *Thuluth* script. The calligraphic ornamentation present in the *masjid* of Imam Muhammad ibn Abdul Wahhab is two-dimensional in its form and is found carved on a number of handcrafted teak doors studded with antique brass. The calligraphy is also depicted and etched on the handles of iron doors. GRC type of calligraphy is placed in the upper part of the *mihrab* as stucco decoration on wall complementing the geometric composition.

4.49
Arabic script of *Qur'an* verses enclosed by circular patterned frame carved on the leaf of purma teak wooden door

4.50
Arabic script of *Qur'an* verses enclosed by rectangular patterned frame carved on the leaf of purma teak wooden door

Conclusion

Epilogue

The Significance of Imam Muhammad ibn Abdul Wahhab Masjid

No one can deny the unprecedented pace of development in contemporary architecture and urbanism in Qatar. In such a distinguished context, adding a new place for relating people to their ideological believes is unquestionably vital and crucial. The significance of the *masjid* is not only in its unique architectural language and visual presence but in the mosque's ability to achieve a balance between traditions and modernity. Symbolically, a mosque is of great importance to Muslims, as it is a worshiper's humble sacred place where daily encounter with God can be established via prayers and physical presence in the mosques' spaces. The *masjid* of Imam Muhammad ibn Abdul Wahhab is undeniably the most impressive religious building in Qatar today. Therefore, it is becoming a national landmark that has engraved its place in people's minds and memories in such a short period of time. It is also arguably one of the most important architectural achievements of contemporary Qatari society. The *masjid* is built in the heart of the city of Doha to serve as a house of prayer and is an ideal place for education spreading the Islamic values in its correct concepts, as well as being a monumental architectural landmark with an outstanding visual reference. Giving the social and cultural responsibility of the mosque, *masjid* of Imam Muhammad ibn Abdul Wahhab is designed in a way that will enhance the performance of such role. Therefore, the *masjid* also functions as a place that:

- propagates the virtues of Islam;
- encourages people looking for a spiritual place where they can be engaged in memorizing the Qur'an;
- educates and raises awareness about some of the contemporary issues and challenges facing Islam through specialized seminars;
- promotes the message of the mosque via regular community events and involvement;
- creates a positive connection with children and the younger generation to come to the mosque and consider it as favorable destination;
- develops number of religious, social, and cultural activities to be hosted in the designated indoor and outdoor spaces.

These functions reveal and enhance the underlying identity of the mosque as the host of social, cultural, and religious events and activities vital to the local community, while imposing the sense of place. Such a

vision for the Imam Muhammad ibn Abdul Wahhab *masjid* is continuously balancing the character and sense of the place with the cultural and social values. The completion of the construction of the *masjid* of Imam Muhammad bin Abdul Wahhab in 2011 supported Qatar's position in the ranks of the Islamic countries focusing on reviving and preserving heritage, local culture, traditions and Islamic identity. Thus, both the Private Engineering Office (POE, the Project proponent) and the Arab Engineering Bureau (AEB, Project Leading Architects, Interior Designers, Construction Supervisors) were keen to build a mosque which would preserve the authentic Qatari architecture and heritage in a simple yet profound manner. Consequently, the design of the *masjid* is inspired by the style of the mosques' design that was popular in the context of traditional settlements and towns of Qatar. The design characteristics of the *masjid* reflect a commitment to maintain a link to the heritage of local mosques while at the same time adequately set the building into the modern developmental context. Such approach creates a sense of continuity and connection to the past, which helps the residents of the community to sustain their ties with the local traditions and culture. This conceptual approach of cultural continuity characterized all the design and construction process of the mosque. Hence, while the mosque is fundamentally inspired by the heritage of the Qatari past, innovative approaches and latest technologies were used in the design of its spaces. Clearly, the vision is to consciously build a consistent connection between past, present and future. With such approach, architecture can credibly claim that it is a catalyst for cultural continuity in the state of Qatar.

The *Masjid*'s Contribution to Qatari Architecture and Local Identity

Architecture and urban historians agree that the most concrete representation of a city's history is its architecture (AlHathlul, 2004; Alraouf, 2011; 2013). The architecture is considered much more than just the physical design of buildings; instead architecture can, in many ways, be viewed as a reflection of the cultural movements of the past. Like any city, Doha has its own unique story to tell, and those stories are told not only through its citizens, but also through its buildings. Preservation of historic traditional architecture and art is imperative to preserving the unique identities of our cities. A concept of multi-domed mosque that went out of fashion in 18th century, made a comeback as Doha embraced its identity through historic preservation of its old-fashioned art. Accordingly, the *masjid* is not only considered as a valuable reference to the old style of architecture and traditional elements of art, but also its monumental presence is a statement to the fast development of Doha's built environment in the modern Qatar by seeing the architecture and urban form as a part of the greater phenomenon of identity being a foundation to the sense of belonging.

Appendix

Glossary

The reader can find here some useful definitions which are distinctive to describe Islamic architecture and design. The list of words and expressions was extended to include specific terminology only related to the context of the Gulf and the state of Qatar.

Adhan
A call to *salat* (prayer), sometimes alternatively spelled and pronounced *azan*, *athan* and *adhan*.

AlMohads
A religious group who founded the fifth Muslim dynasty in the 12th century.

AlMurwab
Name of the fort on the western coast of Qatar, which bears the marks of the Abbasid architectural style.

AlQubeib
Single noun *qubba* (dome), plural *qibab* and *qubeib* (small domes).

AlZubarah
A deserted town located on the north of the Qatar in the Madinat ash Shamal municipality, about 105 km from the Qatar's capital Doha.

Basmala
Also known as *bismillah*, the *basmala* is used extensively in everyday Muslim life, said as the opening of each action in order to receive blessing from God. *Bismillah al-Rahman al-Rahim meaning* "in the name of God, most Gracious, and most merciful."

Bid'ah
In Islam, *bid'ah* refers to any innovations in religious matters.

Courtyard
An open courtyard is the place around which the spaces are organized. The courtyard is usually an area with shade and a source of water to provide humidity. It is also an excellent solution to the privacy needs.

Dir-iyah
Also written as Dereyeh and Dariyya, is a town in Saudi Arabia located on the north-western outskirts of the Saudi capital, Riyadh. Dir-iyah was the original home of the Saudi royal family, and served as the capital of the first Saudi dynasty from 1744 to 1818.

Dome
A dome is a spherical roof structure, with no angles or corners, which encloses a large amount of space. Domes are strong structures, usually in the shape of a hemisphere and sometimes pointed shape.

Eid
Islamic religious holidays and occasions for celebration. Muslims have two such days: the first occurs after the month of fasting and the second in remembrance of the Prophet Abraham (pbuh).

Emir
It is also written as Amir and means ruler or prince.

Emiri Diwan
The governmental headquarters of the State of Qatar.

Eyvan
It is the synonym for the word *riwaq*, a large vaulted hall having one side open to a court. Prevalent in Parthian, Sassanian, and Muslim architecture.

Hadith
It is the collection of teachings and sayings attributed to the Prophet Muhammad (pbuh).

Hajj
The mandatory pilgrimage to Mecca during a predefined period of time. Each Muslim who has the means is required to perform this trip at least once in his/her lifetime.

Haram
The central area for prayer is called a *musalla* or *haram* (literally, "place for prayer").

Imam
Imam is a religious scholar or someone very knowledgeable about Islam who leads the congressional prayers.

Islam
One of today's global religions and the third monotheistic religion, revealed after Judaism and Christianity recognizing them both. Brought by the Prophet Muhammad (570–632) in Arabia, it soon spread all over the southern and eastern Mediterranean,

Africa, and South, East, and Central Asia. In Arabic, the word Islam literally means "to surrender, to submit" (to the will of God), which is the essence of the religion.

Iwan
An *iwan* or in some cases *liwan* is a covered, semi-open space which opens onto the courtyard. It provides a completely shaded area with good ventilation.

Jame'e
A grand, congregational mosque.

Jumaa masjid
A grand, congregational mosque used for Friday communal prayer.

Ka'aba
The cubed looking structure in Mecca toward which all Muslims pray. This is the first house of worship built by Abraham (pbuh) to glorify the Creator of the Universe.

Koranic
It is also written as *Qur'anic*. It means related to or characterized by *Qur'an*.

Madrasa
The word *madrasa* is Arabic for school, and is commonly used throughout the Arab and Islamic world to refer to any place of learning. The specialized institution of learning that was adopted by the Seljuqs to promote Sunni teaching. A *madrasa* usually contains a mosque, classrooms, and lodgings for students and teachers. *Madrasa* first appeared most probably in Khurasan in the 9–10th c. and spread all over the Islamic world in the 11–12th c.

Maqsara
A prayer niche in a mosque or other religious structure, emphasizing the direction of prayer.

Masjid
The place of worship and prayer. Also called "mosque".

Masjid AlShuyoukh
The Arabic name of Qatar Grand Mosque. AlShuyoukh is the plural noun for Sheikh. (The term may be used for the head of an Arab family or of a clan or tribe. It can also mean the chief of an Arab village or a religious official).

Mecca
The sacred city located in Saudi Arabia where Ka'aba is situated. This is also the city where millions of Muslims perform their pilgrimage.

Medina
A city of western Saudi Arabia; the second most holy city of Islam (after Mecca), with the tomb of Prophet Muhammad (pbuh).

Mihrab
Inside the mosque, a niche in one wall, the *mihrab*, indicates the direction of Mecca. Muslims around the world face the direction of Mecca when they pray.

Minaret
A minaret is a tall tower connected to a mosque, from which the call to prayer is given.

Minbar
A raised platform in the front area of a mosque, from which sermons or speeches are given.

Musalla
Generally means place of prayer. Can refer to a small prayer area or to a large open-air space for congregational prayer.

Muslim
The name given to the followers of Islam. This name was first used by Abraham (pbuh), who is recognized as the father of Islam.

Mutawada'a
The place to perform (*wudu*) ablution, the act of washing oneself and the ritual purification in Islam before getting into the prayer hall.

Najd
Najd or Nejd is the central region of Saudi Arabia.

Oyayna
Oyayna, a village located at Yamama in Najd, north-west to the city of Riyadh.

pbuh
Acronym for "Peace Be Upon Him or Her". Used most often in reference to prophets of God.

Phragmites
A non-native, invasive perennial plant with feathery plumes at the top of tall, stiff stalks.

Qibla
The direction of the Ka'aba in Mecca, in modern-day Saudi Arabia. The direction of Mecca toward which Muslims are required to face when they perform their prayer.

Qur'an
The infallible holy book of the Muslims. It contains the word of God in its original form and without any modifications. Refuting one single verse of the Holy *Qur'an* is equivalent to denouncing one's faith.

Rihal
Wooden bookstand used by worshipper while reading *Qur'an*.

Riwaq
An arcade carried on columns or pillars.

Sabeel
In Arabic it means "the way" or a channel or spring of life-giving water.

Ṣaḥīḥ
It is the terminology relating to the authenticity of a *hadith*.

Sahn
An open courtyard usually surrounded by arcades leading to internal spaces.

Salafist
Whom adherents the Salafism, a movement within Sunni Islam whose adherents aim to emulate the practices of the first three generations of Islam, the *salaf*. Salafis consider these first three generations to be exemplary Muslims.

Shamal
The Arabic word of North Direction. Also written as *Ash shamal* or *AlShamal*.

Sheikh
The term used for the head of an Arab family or of a clan or tribe. It can also mean the chief of an Arab village or a religious official.

Sidra
The name Sidra is an Islamic name, short for *Sidrat al-Muntaha*, a holy tree at the end of the seventh heaven.

Sunnah
The way of life prescribed as normative for Muslims on the basis of the teachings and practices of the Islamic prophet Muhammad and interpretations of the *Qur'an*.

Tawhid
The central to Islamic belief means the oneness or unity (in Arabic: *tawhid*) of Allah (God).

Thuluth
Thuluth or *Taliq* script. This type of script with its slender but strongly delineated horizontal and vertical lines, is traditionally used for sacred writing.

Wahhabist
Whom adherents the Salfism movement of Imam Muhammed ibn Abdul Wahhab.

Yamama
The eastern parts of Najid (Saudi Arabia) that are marked by oasis settlements with lots of farming and trading activities, while the rest has traditionally been sparsely occupied by nomadic Bedouins.

Appendix

Bibliography and Selected References

Abdullah, M. 1985
Gypsum Ornamentation in Gulf (1st ed.). Doha: Doha Modern Printing Press.

AlHahtlul, S. 2004
Planning in the Middle East, moving Toward the Future. In: *Habitat International*, Vol. 18, No. 5, pp. 641–43.

AlHathlul, S. 1981
Tradition, Continuity and Change in the Physical Environment: the Arab-Muslim City. Ph.D. dissertation: Massachusetts Institute of Technology.

AlKhulaifi, M.J. 2006
Traditional Architecture in Qatar (2nd ed.). Doha: Ministry of Information and Culture, Department of Tourism and Antiquities.

Alraouf, A.A. 2014
From Mecca to Las Vegas: Critical Notes on Architecture and the Sacred. Cairo: Madarat for Publishing and Research.

Alraouf, A.A. 2013
Doha, A New Emerging Urban Brand – Gulf Cities as Interfaces. The Fourth Gulf Research Meeting. Gulf Research Centre, Cambridge (GRCC) and the University of Cambridge. 2–5 July 2013.

Alraouf, A.A. 2012
A Tale of Two Souqs. In or Out of Place: the Paradox of Gulf Urban Diversity. *Open House International Journal*. Vol. 37, No. 2, June 2012, pp. 72–81.

Alraouf, A.A. 2011
Islam and Arabs, Identity and Globalization: Challenges and Transformations in Contemporary Gulf City. In *Art and Architecture Research and Design Magazine* (Lonaard). London. Vol. 1, No. 4, July 2011, pp. 68–84.

Alraouf, A.A. 2011
Mosquephobia: the Dilemma of Architecture, Multiculturalism and Islam in Art. In *Art and Architecture Research and Design Magazine* (Lonaard). London. Vol. 1, No. 3, May 2011, pp. 78–88.

Baaz, A. (n.d.)
Islamlife.com - Learn About Islam and Muslims - Quran & Sunnah. Retrieved November 11, 2014, from www.islamlife.com/religion2/component/content/article/69-later-scholars/672-biography-of-imam-muhammad-bin-abdul-wahhab

Brend, B. 1992
Islamic Art. Harvard University Press.

Frishman, M. and Kahn, H.-U. (eds.) 1994
The Mosque: History, Architectural Development and Regional Diversity.

Grabar, O. and Ettinghausen, R. 1988
The Art and Architecture of Islam: 650–1250. Viking.

Grabar, O. 1984
From the Past into the Future: On Two Designs for State Mosques. In *Architectural Record*, June 1984.

Hakim, B. 1986
Arabic-Islamic Cities: Building and Planning Principles. London and New York: EmergentCity Press.

Hillenbrand, R. 2004
Islamic Architecture: Form, Function, and Meaning. Columbia University Press.

Hillenbrand, R. 1998
Islamic Art and Architecture. Thames & Hudson.

Holod, R. 1997
Contemporary Mosque. Rizzoli International Publications.

Jaidah, I. and Bourennane, M. 2009
The History of Qatari Architecture from 1800 to 1950. Milano: Skira.

John, F. 2011
Early Ottoman Architecture in Northwestern Anatolia. In *A History of Ottoman Architecture* (1st ed., pp. 43–44). Southampton: WIT Press.

Khadrawi, M. 2009
General Architectural Features of Mosques in Qatar. In *Qatar's Mosques: "History and Architecture"* (1st ed., Vol. 1, pp. 11–27). Doha.

Kuban, D. 1997
Muslim Religious Architecture, part 2: the Development of Religious Architecture in Later Periods, Brill Academic Publishers.

Martin, R.C. (ed.) 2004
Encyclopedia of Islam and the Muslim World, Macmillan.

Mortada, H. 2011
Traditional Islamic Principles of Built Environment. London: Routledge.

Nasr, S.H. 1990
Traditional Islam in the Modern World. London and New York: Routledge.

Nasr, S.H. 1987
Islamic Art and Spirituality. State University of New York Press.

Özkan, S. 1996
Faith, Culture and Architecture. In *Faith and the Built Environment*.

Qatar in the Islamic History (n.d.)
Retrieved January 8, 2015, from www.qatarembassy.net/page/history

Saqqaf, A. (ed.) 1987
The Middle Eastern Cities. New York: Paragon House.

Serageldin, I. 1996
Architecture of the Contemporary Mosque. London: Academy Editions.

Serageldin, I. (ed.) 1989
Space for Freedom. London: Butterworth Architecture.

Sutton, D. 2007
Islamic Design: A Genius For Geometry. New York: Walker Publishing Company Inc.